Leeds' Paintings

20th century British art from Leeds City Art Gallery

Victoria Art Gallery, Bath 23 May–28 June 1980

Huddersfield Art Gallery 5 July–2 August

Herbert Art Gallery & Museum, Coventry 9 August–7 September

Harris Museum & Art Gallery, Preston 13 September–4 October

Booking to be confirmed 25 October–30 November

The Cooper Gallery, Barnsley 6 December–11 January 1981

Usher Gallery, Lincoln 17 January–15 February

Bolton Museum & Art Gallery 21 February–21 March

© Arts Council of Great Britain 1980
ISBN 0 7287 0238 X
Designed by Mike Wade
Printed in England by Balding & Mansell
Exhibition Organiser: Nicola Bennett
Exhibition Assistant: Rowena Gorard

A list of Arts Council publications including
all exhibition catalogues in print, can be
obtained from the Publications Department,
Arts Council of Great Britain, 105 Piccadilly,
London W1V 0AU

Preface

The occasion of this touring exhibition is the closure, for the best part of two years, of Leeds City Art Gallery while work is in progress on their magnificent new extension. To be named the Moore Gallery, in honour of the sculptor, Henry Moore, this building will include a sculpture gallery and an open-air exhibition space on the roof, with a small exhibition gallery and a craft centre below.

With the news that the City Art Gallery would have to close during rebuilding came the thought that there could be no better time to propose a touring exhibition of some of the major works of art belonging to the Gallery. We would like to thank Leeds City Council, represented by the Chairman of the Leisure Services Committee, Councillor Dr Jeffrey Sherwin, and the Director of Art Galleries, Robert Rowe, for their generosity in acceding to our request for the loan of so many fine paintings from the Gallery's collection of twentieth century British art.

We are especially grateful to Miranda Strickland-Constable, Keeper of the collection, for selecting the works and writing the catalogue for *Leeds' Paintings*— making an exhibition which not only demonstrates the character of this important collection but which also gives a thoughtful and coherent picture of the course of British painting during this century. We would like to thank Alex Robertson, Assistant Keeper, for all his help.

Joanna Drew
Director of Art

The Leeds City Art Gallery Collection

In making this selection of paintings and other works of art from the Leeds Art Gallery collections, we have restricted the choice to British art of the twentieth century, because it is an area in which we feel particularly well-endowed, and it seemed possible to put together an exhibition with a coherent theme, rather than a haphazard grouping of 'treasures'.

We have chosen for the most part works which, at the time they were made, counted as 'avant-garde', and it is a matter of some pride that many of these works were acquired soon after they were produced. The collecting of modern art as a matter of avowed policy goes back at least to the appointment of Frank Rutter as Curator in 1912 – though it should be noted that before that at least one of the Art Gallery's patrons, Sam Wilson (for a number of years a member of the Art Gallery Committee), was well aware that the outsize exhibition productions of Royal Academicians did not represent all that was best in British art and saw to it that the Art Gallery reaped the benefit of his beliefs.

Painting and sculpture in Britain in the twentieth century have been of an inventive-ness not previously observed in this country's arts since the Middle Ages. While never wholeheartedly succumbing to the 'isms' wafting over from Europe and, later, America there have been enough jolts and infusions to create an overall sense of vitality. Influences from abroad have been important enough to British artists for it to be possible to write the history of art here in this century almost entirely in terms of its reflections of these influences. This, though difficult to avoid, is also rather unfair to the artists concerned, who were working in Britain and in the context of a British audience, and who were often seriously concerned to reach that audience (the Camden Town painters are a case in point).

Here is not the place to discuss at length the 'Britishness' or otherwise of British art, but the question is relevant, since we are discussing the formation of a public collection, and the matter of taste is very important here. An artist does not make paintings and sculpture according to the canons of taste but according to the dictates of his thoughts, ideas, feelings. It is the collector who exercises taste, and even in a collection built up over a number of years by several different curators, members of committees, and kind benefactors it will be seen to operate. (Even these latter do not, unless, like Sam Wilson, they give an entire collection, fundamentally change the character of a museum much, since most donors of one or two cherished pictures, will choose to give them to a collection which will provide an appropriate context, where they will hang happily with the other works on show.)

It is difficult when one has worked with a collection of pictures for over ten years to be able to assess its precise character – it has become too familiar – but one or two gaps will be observed in the Leeds collection, to people familiar with the history of the period. Vorticism for instance is not represented by a painting (though we have some prints and a splendid Bomberg drawing, not in the exhibition). Similarly, one would not guess from this exhibition, what a stir the Surrealists made in England in 1936 – the reflections of the movement in the works of Nash and Wadsworth, for instance, are rather gentle examples. And in works after 1960 there is a bias towards abstract painting. Nevertheless, Leeds was one of the first public galleries outside London to buy a painting by Francis Bacon, and with certain aspects, at least, of art since 1950 we hope we have 'kept up'.

Paintings of the sixties were often very large in size, and we have decided regretfully, not to include such works in this exhibition for fear of 'unbalancing' it and creating practical difficulties on tour. After 1960, therefore, only small-scale works are included.

I would like to thank the authors of works listed at the end of the catalogue under 'Further Reading', and also authors of more specialised books, too numerous to mention, on whose work I have drawn in writing the text.

The Background — *British art movements in the twentieth century*

In the later nineteenth century the Royal Academy's dominating position in British art was challenged by the opening of several private galleries, and also by the foundation of a new exhibiting society – the New English Art Club, where younger artists, notably Philip Wilson Steer and other enthusiasts of the French Impressionists and plein-air painters could show work unacceptable in the older institution.

By 1905, however, the N.E.A.C. had become in its turn part of the Establishment; several members were themselves R.A.'s, and younger artists found it difficult to get their work accepted. During the next 10 years, a number of smaller and less formal groups were formed. Walter Sickert (who had returned in 1905 from an extended period of residence in France) started the Fitzroy Street Group in 1907. A house was taken in Fitzroy Street in Camden Town where members could meet and show recent work to each other and to prospective buyers and interested friends. Spencer Gore and Harold Gilman belonged to this group; among their commonly held beliefs were a liking for small pictures of domestic subjects – or views of the urban life they saw around them – without the staginess or the story-telling still common in Academy paintings, painted in a style which was a sober English variety of Impressionism. A much larger organisation was the Allied Artists' Association; founded by the art critic

Frank Rutter, it held annual exhibitions for as many artists as possible, with no selection jury.

A more exclusive group was the Friday Club (1905), led by Vanessa Bell and Duncan Grant, with Roger Fry the chief champion of modern French painting in England before 1920. The advances of Post-Impressionism, especially the work of Gauguin, Van Gogh and Cezanne, and, to a smaller extent, Matisse and Picasso were celebrated in the exhibition at the Grafton Galleries in 1910 of *Manet and the Post-Impressionists* organised by Roger Fry. Much of the painting was too 'advanced' for Sickert, but his younger associates soon brightened their palettes and simplified their form to take account of the new expressive power of colour. The Camden Town Group, perhaps because it has given its name to the style of painting led by Gore and Gilman, described above – and perhaps also by association with Sickert's Camden Town Murder pictures which shocked critics on account of their 'sordid' subject-matter – is the best known of these societies. (It was also the shortest-lived, being dissolved and re-constituted as the London group in 1913, after two years of existence.) Led by Sickert, Gilman and Gore, it included Charles Ginner, Malcolm Drummond, Augustus John, Innes, Duncan Grant, and most strangely, Wyndham Lewis, later founder of the Rebel Art Centre and self-proclaimed leader of the

more aggressively avant-garde Vorticists who included Edward Wadsworth, C.R.W. Nevinson and William Roberts. The Camden Town Group was making a serious attempt to open its doors to progressive artists (whether or not of their own persuasion) while maintaining what they felt to be a high standard.

It is relevant to the present exhibition to note that the art critic Frank Rutter, acquainted particularly with the Camden Town Group but with a knowledge of the newer French art and a keen champion of modernism, became the second Curator of Leeds Art Gallery in 1912, and made a serious effort through lecturing and organising exhibitions, to put the Leeds art-loving public in touch with newer work (the regular loan exhibitions in Leeds had previously been graced chiefly by paintings from last year's Royal Academy). With the encouragement of Sir Michael Sadler, newly appointed Vice Chancellor of Leeds University and himself a keen collector of modern art, Frank Rutter founded the Leeds Art Collections Fund (an early example of a 'Friends of the Art Gallery' society) which aimed to raise money for the purchase of works of art for the collection – with a particular emphasis on new art. While at Leeds Frank Rutter found time to organise an important exhibition of new art in 1913 at the Doré Galleries in London, which included work by Gilman, Ginner, Gore, Wyndham

Lewis, Sickert, Epstein, Nevinson, Wadsworth, Lucien Pissarro and Malcolm Drummond (to quote only those represented in the present exhibition).

Vorticist art made a far more radical break with the past than anything produced by the Camden Town painters or even by Vanessa Bell or Duncan Grant, whose experiments in abstraction were more cheerfully decorative and thus more accessible. Wyndham Lewis, Wadsworth, Roberts and C.R.W. Nevinson were by the early years of the First World War making drawings and paintings that were nearly or sometimes wholly abstract, in a highly conceptualised, faceted style based on Cubism and Italian Futurism, with a propagandist fervour clearly characterised by the title of their magazine BLAST.

In 1913, then, with the Camden Town Group and Vorticism, London seemed to have a genuinely avant-garde movement for the first time. The outbreak of war, however, broke the momentum which had been growing. The war itself produced some memorable painting – under the War Artists Scheme Wyndham Lewis and Paul Nash produced powerful work, and Nevinson's war paintings are surely his best – but with the return of peace some kind of pause seems to have been a necessity with most artists. During the 1920's not only the younger artists, Stanley Spencer, Paul Nash, Mark

Gertler and the other painters who had been members of a remarkable generation of students at the Slade School of Art before the war, but also artists like Epstein, Wadsworth and Roberts who had taken part in the 'movements' of the pre-war years, followed now differing and individual paths.

Stanley Spencer had his own vision of things, and set his strangely formed Biblical characters in the landscape of his own village of Cookham. Paul Nash pursued an overtly romantic course but like Burra and, later, Wadsworth, was susceptible to the influence of Surrealism which he encountered in France. By the 1930's, however, the post-war modern movements in Germany, France and the Netherlands were affecting British architecture and design as well as painting and sculpture. Henry Moore, Barbara Hepworth and Ben Nicholson were the leading modernists, prepared to accept abstract forms as a necessary alternative to naturalistic images. As before the war, groups and societies were formed, the most important perhaps being the Seven and Five Society (founded in 1919) led in its later years by Ben Nicholson – around 1930 its members included Frances Hodgkins and Christopher Wood and in 1935 it held the first all-abstract exhibition in England, at which among others Henry Moore, Barbara Hepworth, Ben Nicholson, John Piper and Ivon Hitchens showed work. Paul Nash also instituted a

shorter-lived society called Unit One (including Nash, Moore, Hepworth, Nicholson, Tristram Hillier and others) who published an important collection, edited by Herbert Read, of statements and illustrations by all the members, who included architects as well as painters and sculptors.

A more remarkable feature of this period (compared to twenty years earlier) was the adherence of several British artists to Continental societies such as Abstraction-Creation, whose 40 members included Arp, Calder, Gabo and Moholy-Nagy, with England represented by Barbara Hepworth, Ben Nicholson and Edward Wadsworth. Altogether there was far more coming and going between the Continent – especially Paris – during the thirties than before the First World War.

In 1936 a major international exhibition of Surrealist Art took place in London. Surrealism, with its emphasis on imagination and the role of the unconscious in the shaping of fantasy, acted as an opposing force to the rationalist ideals of the Constructive (i.e. abstract) artists; more than one artist accepted ideas from both camps, the work of Paul Nash being the most striking example.

Most of the leading artists of the day were invited by Philip Hendy, Director from 1935 to 1945, to show their work in Leeds in a remarkable series of one- and two-man exhibitions at the City Art Gallery. When the Gallery closed with the outbreak of war the exhibitions were continued at Temple Newsam House, five miles from the City centre. Works were often acquired for the permanent collection from these exhibitions – examples in the present show are Ben Nicholson's *Painting 1940* and Ivon Hitchens' *Hazel Wood* – for besides the support of the Leeds Art Collections Fund, the Art Gallery had now a regular purchase fund from the City Council, granted in 1937 under the Chairmanship of Alderman Percival Leigh.

During the Second World War a War Artists Scheme was set up, giving many artists the opportunity to produce work on a regular contract basis, under the terms of which the paintings and drawings were accepted by the Government and distributed after the cessation of hostilities to public collections all over the country. Henry Moore, John Piper and Graham Sutherland all worked for this scheme.

During the 1950's, the most striking change to be seen was the shift of the centre of the international art scene from Paris to New York. The rise of a new school of American painters, whose work could be seen in England from the mid-fifties on, was welcomed especially by the painters – Peter Lanyon, Terry Frost, Patrick Heron and

others – who had settled in St Ives, on the Cornish coast, who themselves were moving towards an abstract art which was freer, more expressive and on a larger scale than the more architectural abstraction of the thirties. Abstract expressionism, colour field painting and, later, Pop Art (in which the British can be said to have led the field) all had their counterparts in this country ; artists of the younger generation – Richard Smith, John Walker – spent long and fruitful periods working in New York early in their careers.

A special feature of the Leeds collection is the inclusion of works by artists who have held Gregory Fellowships in Painting and Sculpture at Leeds University. These Fellowships, founded by Peter Gregory in 1950, are the earliest established 'Artist-in-Residence' posts in this country – they provided for an artist the opportunity for a year or two to work at his own painting or sculpture without the necessity to teach in order to earn a living. Alan Davie, Terry Frost, Hubert Dalwood, John Walker and Keith Milow are the artists represented in this exhibition who have held these posts.

During the seventies, many artists returned to work on a smaller scale – there was a rising belief that more portable works were more accessible, less 'expensive-looking' (there had come about a distaste for the idea that great art equals great money). The kind of art

sometimes known as 'conceptual' does away with the notion of artist as a craftsman making a precious object – Richard Long for instance makes sculptures either in a gallery or in the landscape itself, from natural materials, stones, tree branches and so on. When these are presented to the public in photographic form Long is able to involve ideas of time and space, not available in previous art in quite the same way.

It is difficult, because we are dealing with the present time, of which our view is more confused than that of the past, to tell how the more recent areas of the collection will look to our successors – no doubt they too will find gaps needing to be filled – but we feel it important to continue the Leeds tradition of collecting right up to the present day ; for the curator art-collecting should not be just a question of backing the right horses, it should be a commitment to the changing response of the artist to a changing world.

Miranda Strickland-Constable

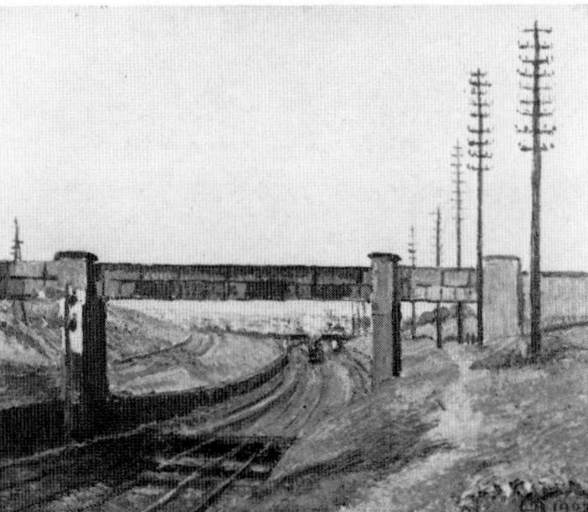

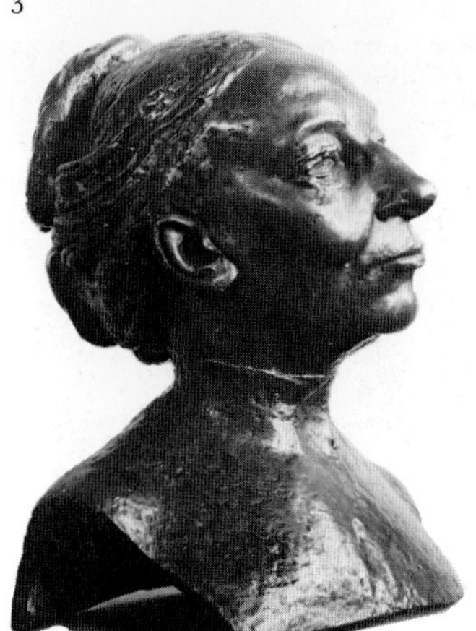

1 **Philip Wilson Steer** 1860–1942
Poole Harbour 1890
oil on canvas $18\frac{1}{2} \times 24\frac{1}{2}$ in $(45\cdot7 \times 62\cdot2$ cm$)$
signed and dated

Philip Wilson Steer was an early member of
the New English Art Club, founded in 1886
(Sickert joined it two years later) which aimed
at providing an alternative venue to the Royal
Academy for showing the work of younger
artists. Steer, who had spent some time in
France, was the centre of a progressive group
of these younger artists. *Poole Harbour* is one
of the works of this period which
demonstrate his freshness of vision, his ability
to subsume minor details into an overall
impression of suffused light, albeit softer,
more tentative and 'English' in manner than
his French mentors.

*Formerly in the collection of Edward Marsh; given
by the Contemporary Art Society, 1954*

2 **Lucien Pissarro** 1863–1944
Wells Farm Bridge, Acton 1907
oil on canvas $18 \times 21\frac{1}{2}$ in $(45\cdot7 \times 54\cdot5$ cm$)$
signed and dated

Exhibited in 1907 at the New English Art
Club and subsequently at the Camden Town
Group, 1911. This was the first modern
painting bought by the newly formed Leeds
Art Collections Fund in 1913. Railway
subjects were favoured by the French
Impressionists (of whom Lucien's father,
Camille Pissarro, was a leading member) as
being particularly typical of modern urban
life, a theme central to the beliefs of the
Camden Town painters.

Given by the Leeds Art Collections Fund, 1925

3 **Jacob Epstein** 1880–1959
Portrait of Lady Gregory 1911
bronze h. 15 in (38 cm)

Augusta Gregory, 1852–1932, Irish
dramatist, with W.B. Yeats founded the
Abbey Theatre in Dublin, where the plays of
Yeats and Syngè and other works particularly
connected with Irish myth and history were
presented. Lady Gregory's nephew Sir Hugh
Lane, who commissioned the bust, thought it
made his aunt look too fierce, but Epstein had
been determined to present his sitter as the
serious, intellectual lady he saw her to be.

Bought 1942

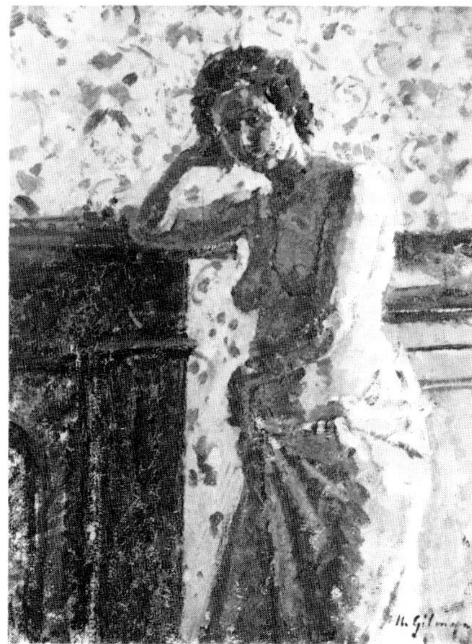

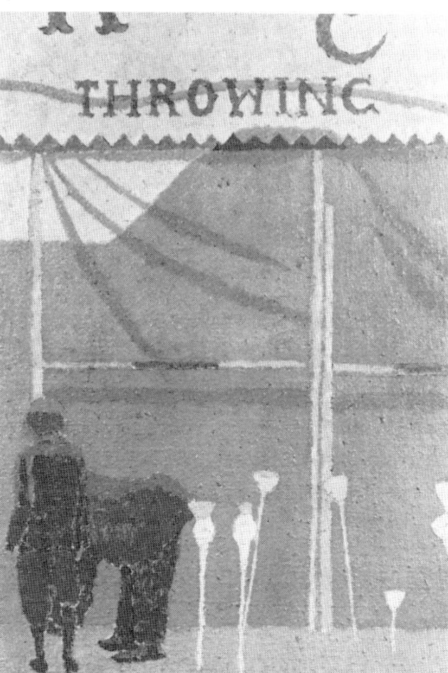

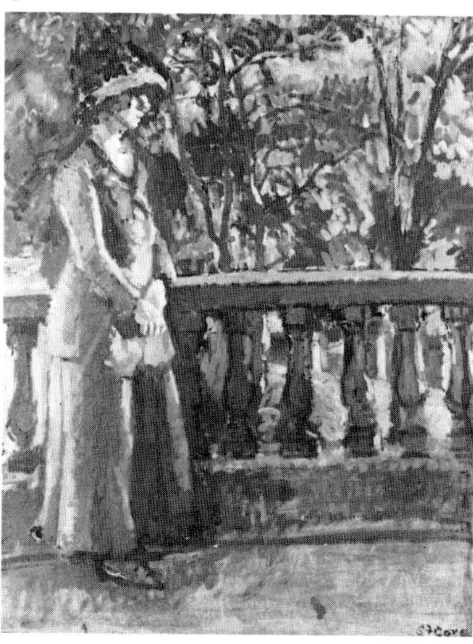

4 **Harold Gilman** 1876–1919
Interior with nude c. 1911
oil on canvas 20 × 16 in (50·8 × 40·6 cm)
signed

This is a painting in a light, colourful,
impressionistic style with broken touches,
painted perhaps c. 1911–12, and showing the
influence of Gilman's Camden Town friends,
especially Gore. It is characteristic of Gilman
that the nude here though seen in a domestic
interior seems posed for a painting, not
caught at a moment of everyday life, in the
usual 'Camden Town' manner – she is dressed
(if that is the word) like the Venus de Milo. It
originally belonged to Charles Ginner.

Bought 1949

5 **Malcolm Drummond** 1880–1945
The Coconut Shy c. 1911–12
oil on canvas 19 × 13 in (48·2 × 33 cm)

Members of the Camden Town Group were
committed to using their own everyday
surroundings as subject-matter and these
included the jollier aspects of London
life – music halls (see no. 13), circuses and
fairgrounds were favourite subjects. This
painting by one of the lesser-known members
of the group is remarkable for the bold and
decorative use of the lettered sign across the
upper part of the picture.

Bought 1970

6 **Spencer Gore** 1878–1914
The Balcony, Mornington Crescent 1911
oil on canvas 24 × 20 in (60·9 × 50·8 cm)

Spencer Gore lived at 31 Mornington
Crescent in the Camden Town area until his
marriage, in January 1912, to Mary Johanna
Kerr, the girl standing on the balcony in this
sun-drenched landscape. The opposition of
vivid greens and violet-blues was often found
in Gore's painting; the handling, in small
patches of freely brushed paint, is still in a
more or less Impressionist manner.

Bought 1949

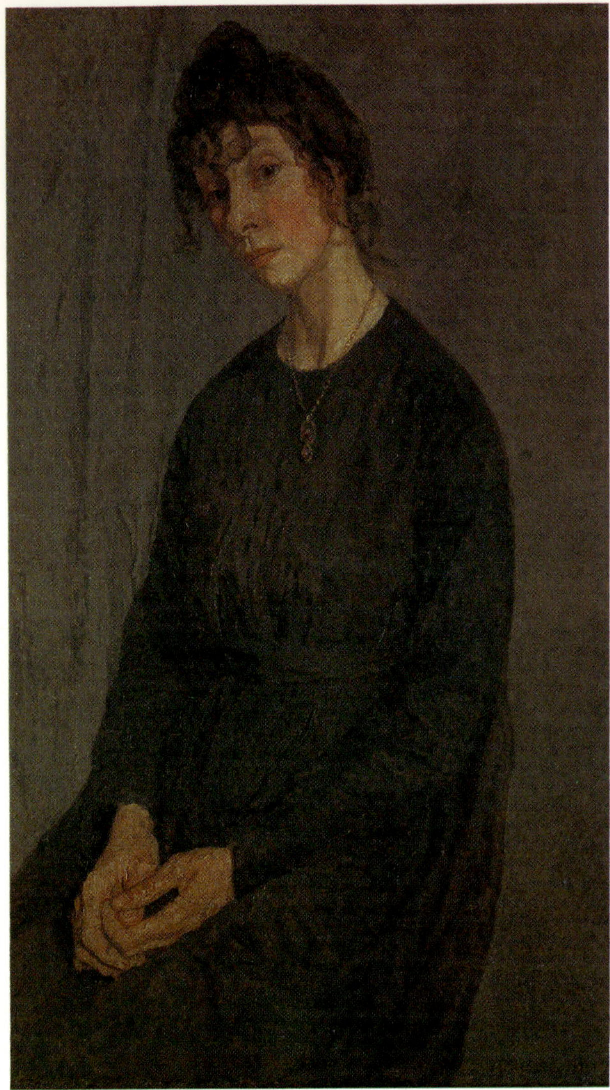

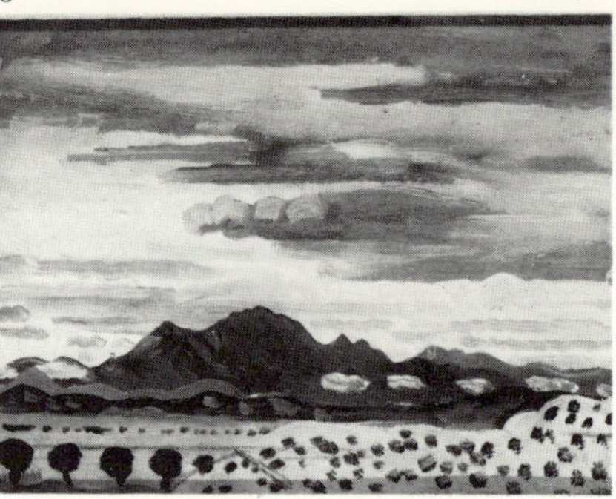

7 **Gwen John** 1876–1939
Portrait of Chloë Boughton-Leigh c. 1910
oil on canvas 23¾ × 15 in (60·3 × 38·6 cm)

Chloë was the sister of a painter friend of
Gwen John's, Maude Boughton-Leigh, with
whom she had studied on the Continent.
Later the sisters went to live on Canvey
Island, where they took up social work. At
least two other portraits of Chloë by Gwen
John are known (Tate Gallery, Birmingham).
This version was sold to the American
collector, John Quinn, in August 1914, but
Gwen John may have been working on it in
September–October 1910.

Bought 1955

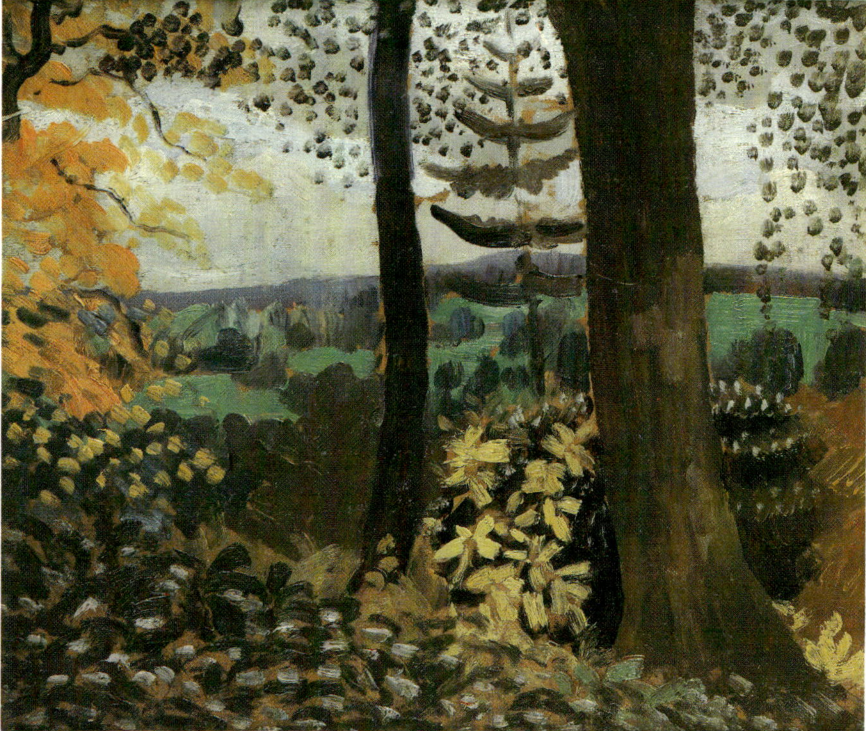

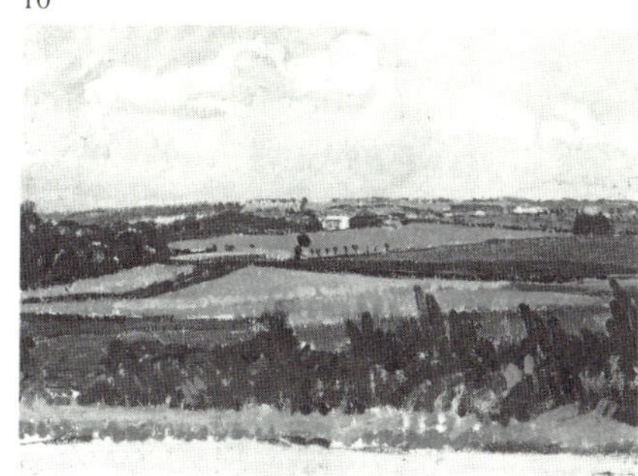

8 **James Dickson Innes** 1887–1914
In the Pyrenees c. 1911
oil on panel $9\frac{1}{2} \times 13$ in ($24\cdot2 \times 33$ cm)

During Innes's last years he was suffering from tuberculosis (from which he died at the age of 27) and spent much time in the South of France, painting the Pyrenees instead of his beloved Welsh mountains. His style was quite individual–small landscapes in which a rich and subtle combination of colours was brushed on to the surface in a fluid technique not unlike a wash drawing.

The view is of the foothills of the Pyrenees to the west of Collioure.

Given by A.E. Anderson, 1929

9 **Augustus John** 1878–1961
Landscape at Chirk c. 1912
oil on panel 13×16 in ($33 \times 40\cdot6$ cm)

In 1912 Augustus John visited Wales with J.D. Innes. They stayed near Arenig, and on the back of this panel is a view of that mountain. John went on to Chirk Castle to paint a portrait of Lady Howard de Walden. The technique with its dots and dashes in bright colours is as close as John ever got to Innes's style. The picture is related also to the small, brilliantly coloured landscapes John was painting during these years in the South of France and in Dorset.

Given by H.M. Hepworth, 1934

10 **Spencer Gore** 1878–1914
In Berkshire c. 1912
oil on canvas $15\frac{1}{4} \times 21$ in ($38\cdot6 \times 53\cdot2$ cm)

In the summer of 1912 Harold Gilman lent his house at Letchworth in Hertfordshire to Spencer Gore and his wife. Gore thus spent a concentrated period painting landscapes and it seems to be at this time that he began to develop a new style–the shimmer of leaves in sunlight of no. 7 is gradually replaced by flat, simplified planes in more arbitrary-seeming colours, violets, blue-greens, pinks and oranges, never becoming actually strident, but handled with all Gore's own particular sensitivity.

Bought 1936

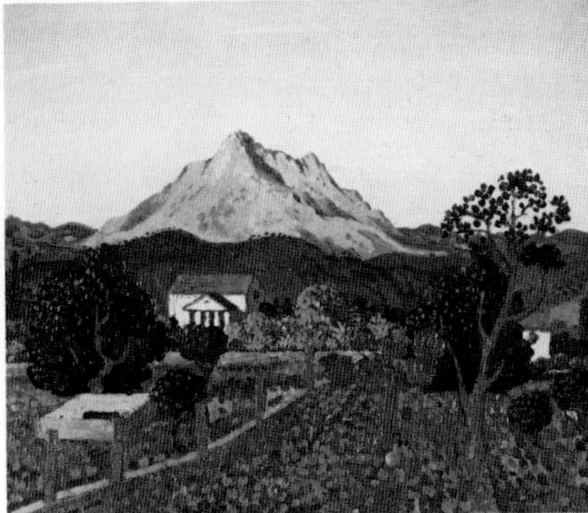

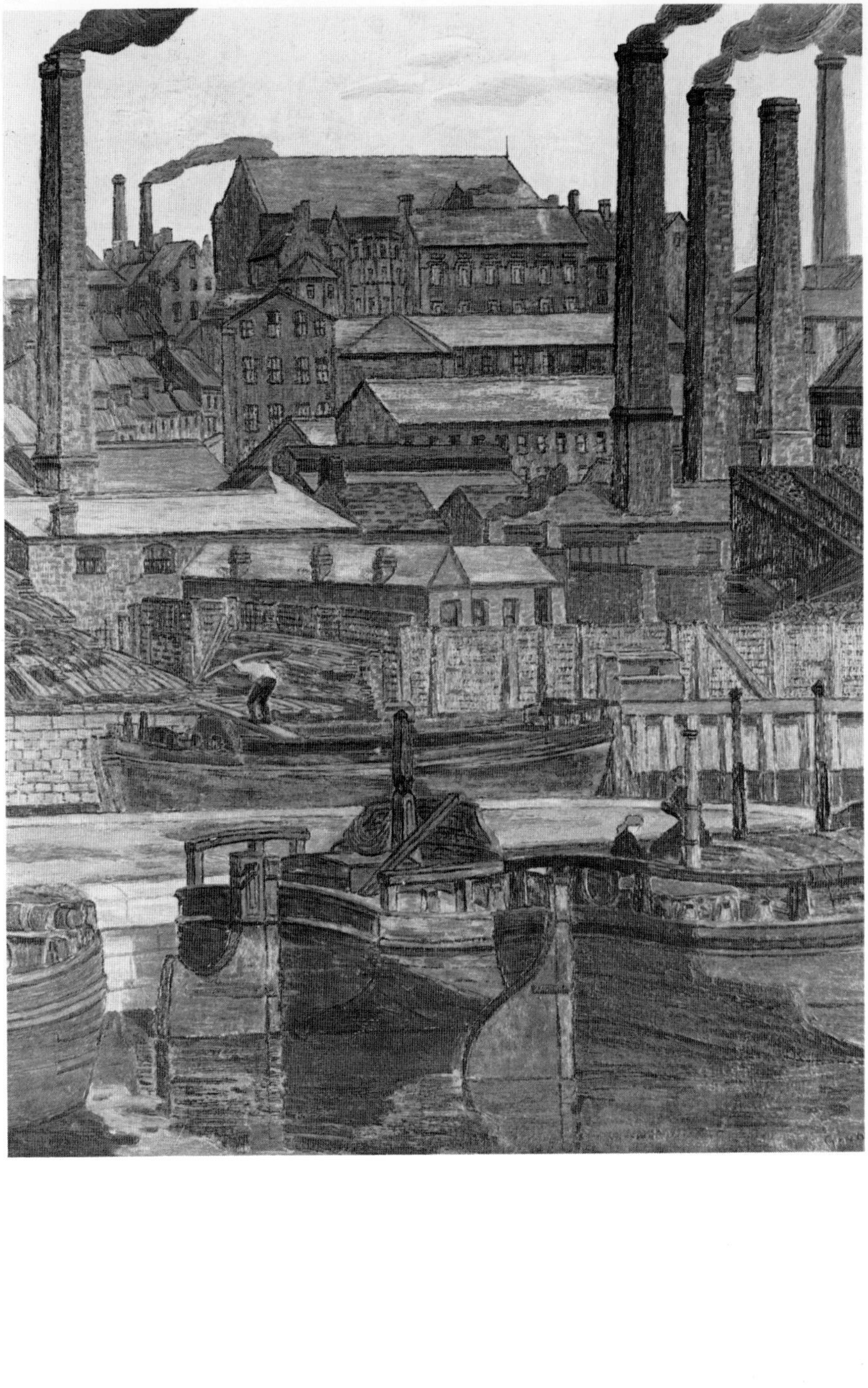

11 **Derwent Lees** 1885–1931
The Little Gardens, 1913
oil on panel 13 × 16 in (33 × 40·6 cm)
signed and dated

Derwent Lees spent the winter of 1912/13
painting in the South of France with J.D.
Innes, and this painting shows the influence
of Innes's style, especially in the small spots of
colour used by Innes as a kind of shorthand
for trees and bushes. Lees has used this
method extensively, making for a rather
'busier' effect than Innes would have
produced.

Bequeathed by H.M. Hepworth, 1943

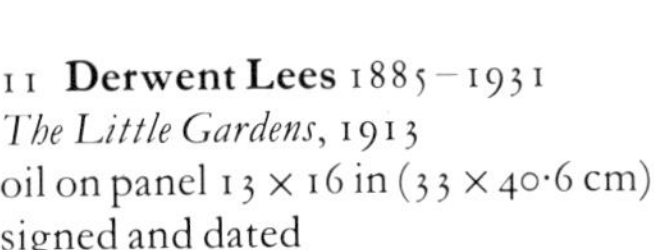

12 **Charles Ginner** 1878–1952
Leeds Canal 1914
oil on canvas 29 × 23 in (73·6 × 58·4 cm)
signed

Charles Ginner's basic liking for realism
shows in the subdued colours of this subject.
His was a carefully studied kind of realism
entailing both a thorough involvement with
his subject, and a sound craftsmanlike
approach to the practice of painting. Both
Ginner and Gilman advocated this approach,
which they called 'Neo-Realism'. Ginner
probably painted this on a visit to Frank
Rutter, curator of Leeds Art Gallery from
1912–17. It was exhibited at the Goupil
Gallery in 1914.

Given by Mrs R. Caldicott, 1962

13 **Walter Richard Sickert** 1860–1942
The New Bedford c. 1915–16
oil & tempera on canvas 73 × 28½ in
(185·5 × 72·4 cm)

The New Bedford Music Hall in Camden
Town was built to replace the 'Old' Bedford
which had been burnt down in 1899. Sickert
was fond of music-halls as subjects; this
composition seems to have been first painted
by him around 1906–7. He used it again when
the painter, Ethel Sands, commissioned him
to do decorations on music-hall themes for
her dining-room. The Leeds picture is the
only one which was finished. The music-hall
as a theme allowed Sickert to combine his
own love for the theatre with his belief that
pictures should take the everyday for their
subject.

Bought 1937

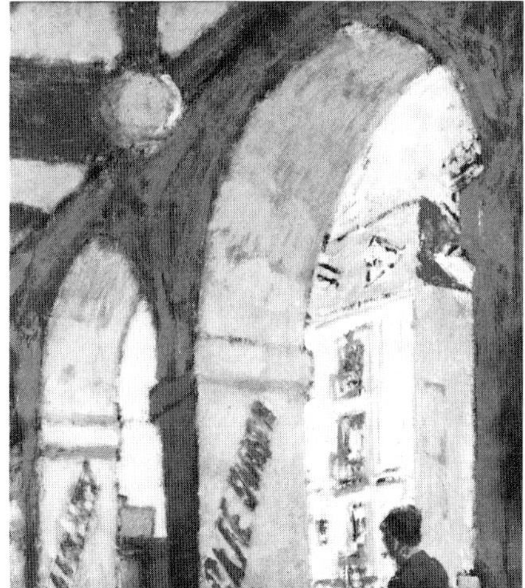

14 **Walter Richard Sickert** 1860–1942
Café des Arcades (The Café Suisse, Dieppe)
c. 1914
oil on canvas 21 × 15 in (53·3 × 38·1 cm)
signed

Probably painted during the summer Sickert
spent near Dieppe just before the outbreak of
war, this painting is in light tones and varied
colours, the sunlight through the arches
playing an important part in the composition
but off-set by luminous coloured shadows
instead of the stark *contre-jour* effects of
Sickert's strictly Camden Town paintings.
Dieppe was Sickert's favourite summer
painting place in these years; earlier on, he
had actually lived there for some time.

Bought 1942

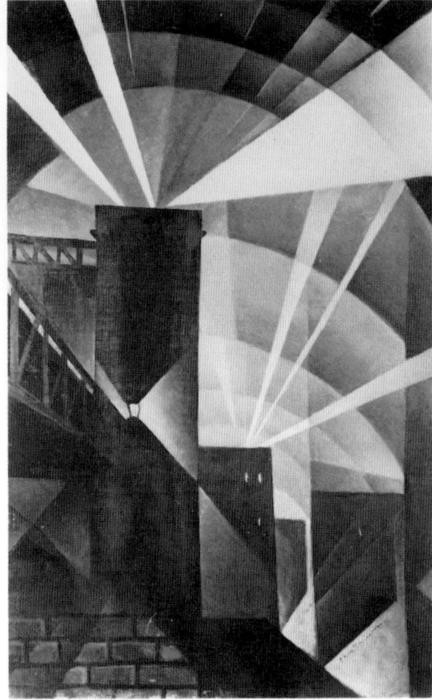

15

16

15 Christopher Richard Wynne Nevinson
1889–1946
Searchlights 1915
oil on canvas 24 × 16 in (60·9 × 40·6 cm)
signed

Another view of a railway bridge (like no. 2);
it almost has the force of a symbol of the
modern world. For Nevinson this is
especially true–he was an admirer of the
Italian Futurists, especially Marinetti, for
whom the machine age represented the future
in art as in life. Furthermore this is a war
picture; painted in 1915 it shows the
searchlights on Hungerford Bridge at
Charing Cross, and was shown in Nevinson's
exhibition of *Paintings of War* in the following
year.

*Given anonymously to the Leeds Art Collections
Fund, 1928*

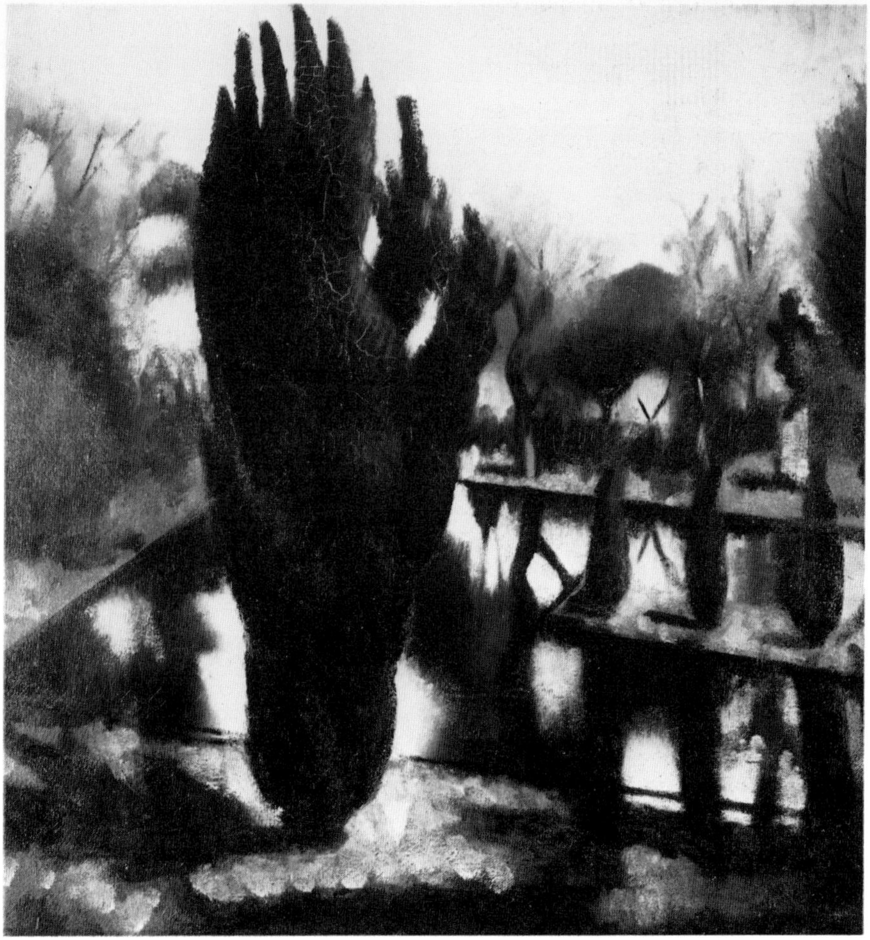

16 Mark Gertler 1891–1939
The Pond 1916
oil on canvas 25 × 25 in (63·3 × 63·3 cm)
signed and dated

A view of the pond at Garsington Manor,
Oxfordshire, the home of Philip and Ottoline
Morrell, whose hospitality offered to artists
and writers was never more welcome than
during the war years, when those of pacifist
persuasion, like Mark Gertler, often stayed
for long periods. Gertler, a struggling young
artist at the time, had his own studio in a
nearby cottage.

Bought 1941

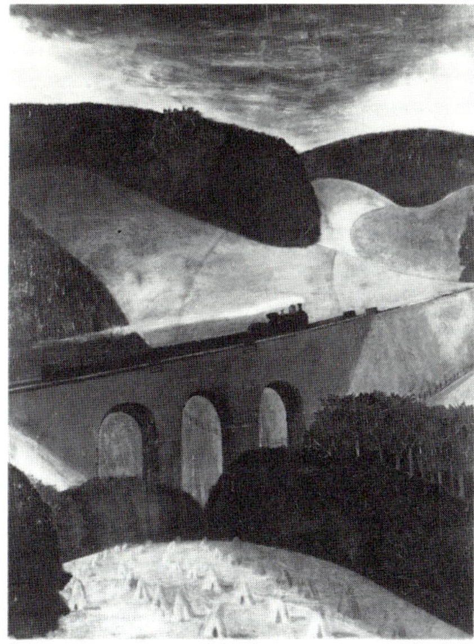

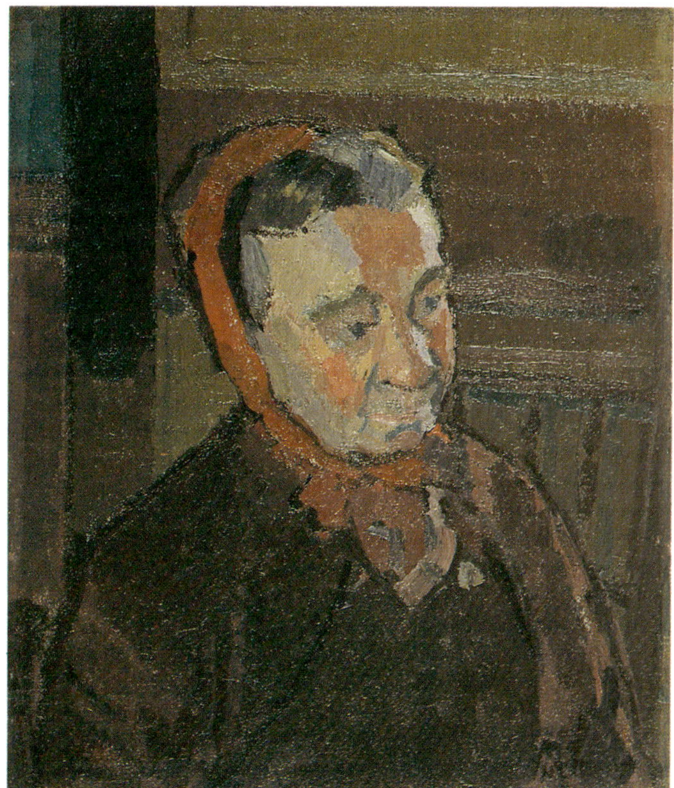

17 **John Nash** 1893–1977
The Viaduct 1916
oil on canvas 35 × 26 in (88·8 × 66 cm)

This is an early work by Nash, first exhibited
at the London Group (successor to the
Camden Town Group) in 1916 when he was
23. In its attempt to simplify and flatten the
shapes seen in the landscape it shows a
tendency towards modernism which John
(unlike his elder brother Paul) was later to
discard in favour of a more traditional
landscape style.

Bought 1940

18 **Harold Gilman** 1876–1919
Mrs Mounter c. 1916–17
oil on canvas 13 × 17 in (33 × 17·9 cm)
signed

In Harold Gilman's last years (he died in the
1919 influenza epidemic aged 43) he was
president of the London Group (the enlarged
society which grew from an enlarged and
reconstituted Camden Town Group). He was
breaking away from the English version of
Impressionism which had characterised his
work during the Camden Town years,
towards a more formal style, using brighter
colours in broader, more clearly defined
planes. Mrs Mounter was Gilman's
housekeeper – this small work is probably a
preliminary study for the well-known *Mrs
Mounter at the Breakfast Table* in the Walker
Art Gallery, Liverpool.

Bought 1934

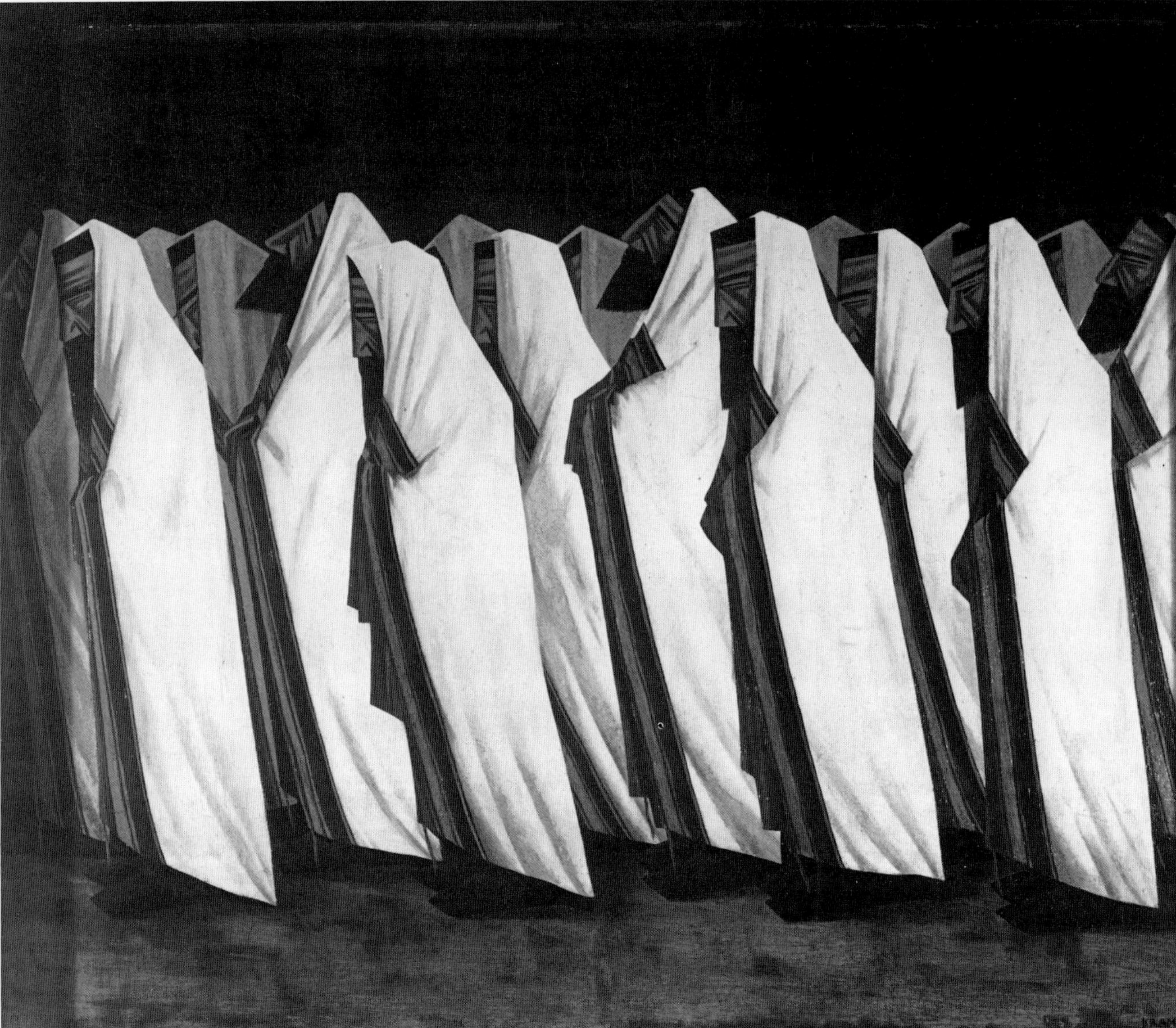

19 **Jacob Kramer** 1892–1962
The Day of Atonement 1919
oil on canvas 39 × 48 in (99 × 121·9 cm)
signed and dated

Jacob Kramer was born in the Ukraine but
grew up as part of the Jewish community in
Leeds and in many of his earlier paintings
shows a preoccupation with Jewish subject-
matter. In London he was attracted to the
circle of artists around Wyndham Lewis and
the magazine *BLAST*. Kramer has used the
flat, angular drawing derived ultimately from
Cubism, favoured by Lewis and Bomberg,
together with an almost primitive repetition
of the figures – to point up the ritual and
emotional elements in his subject – Jews
praying in Synagogue on Yom Kippur.

Given by the Jewish Community in Leeds, 1920

20 **Percy Wyndham Lewis** 1882–1957
Praxitella 1920
oil on canvas 56 × 40 in (142·2 × 101·6 cm)
signed

Wyndham Lewis included this painting in an
exhibition, mainly of portraits, which he held
at the Leicester Galleries in 1921.

This highly stylised portrait, like others in
that exhibition, is on the scale of life and
retains something of the prophetic Lewis of
the Vorticist movement and *BLAST*
magazine, more so than the more
conventional though often very beautiful
portrait drawings Lewis did to commission
during the twenties and thirties. The steely
beauty who sat for this painting was Iris
Barry, who founded the first London Film
Society in 1925 and was in charge of the Film
Library of the Museum of Modern Art, New
York, from 1935.

*Given by Edward Wadsworth through the
Contemporary Art Society, 1945*

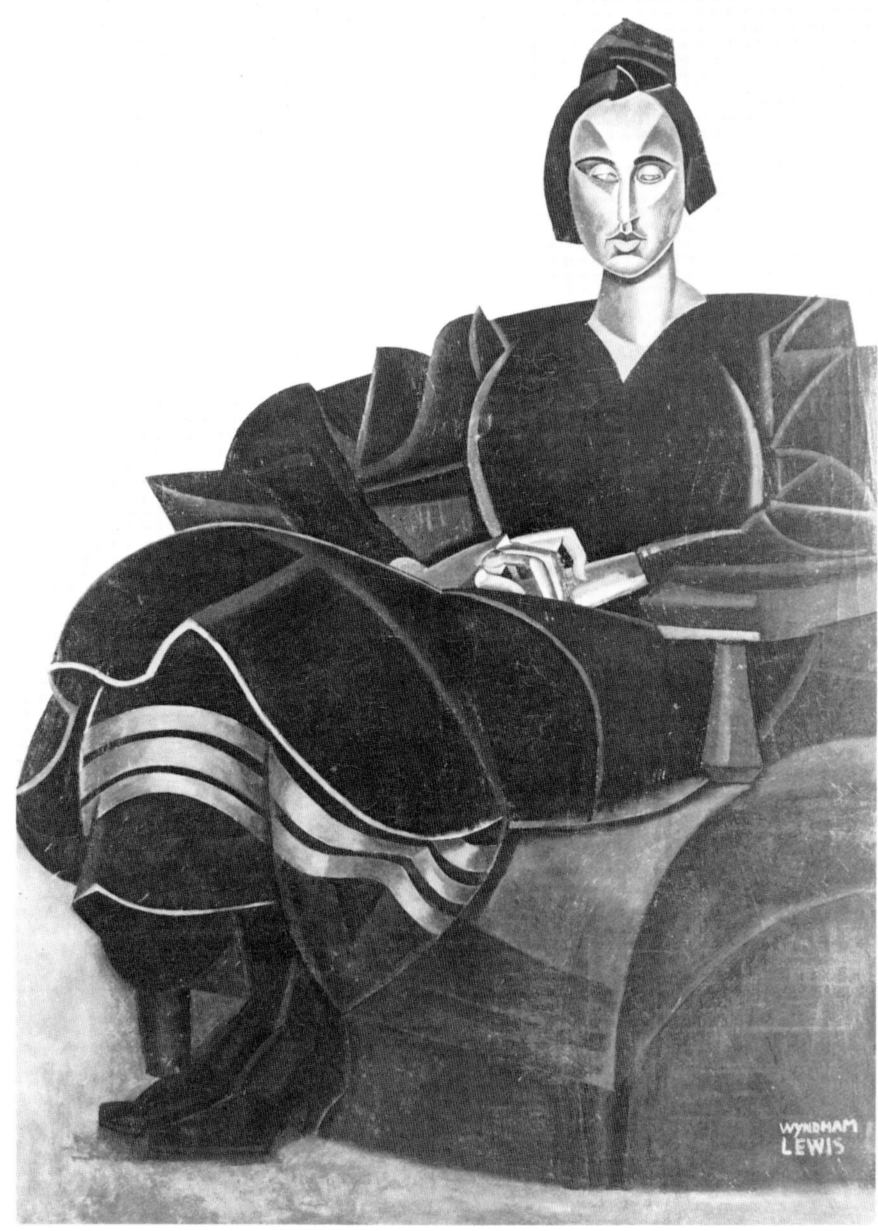

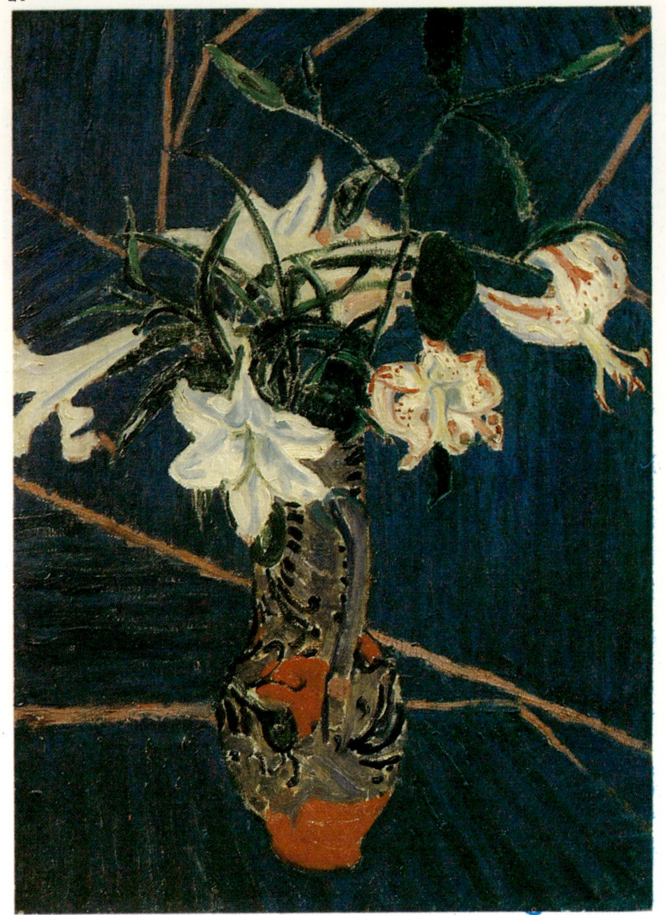

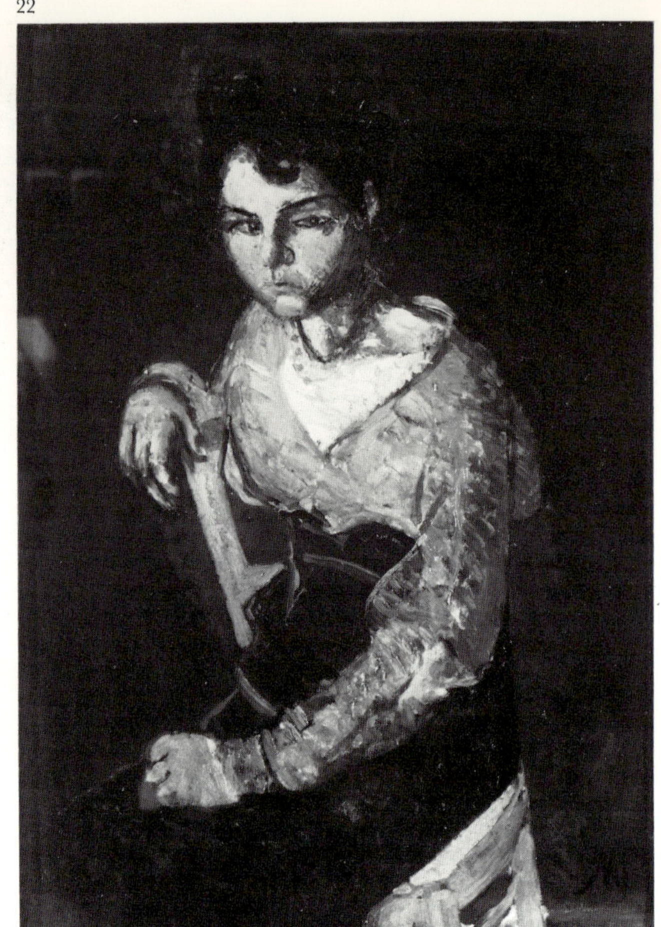

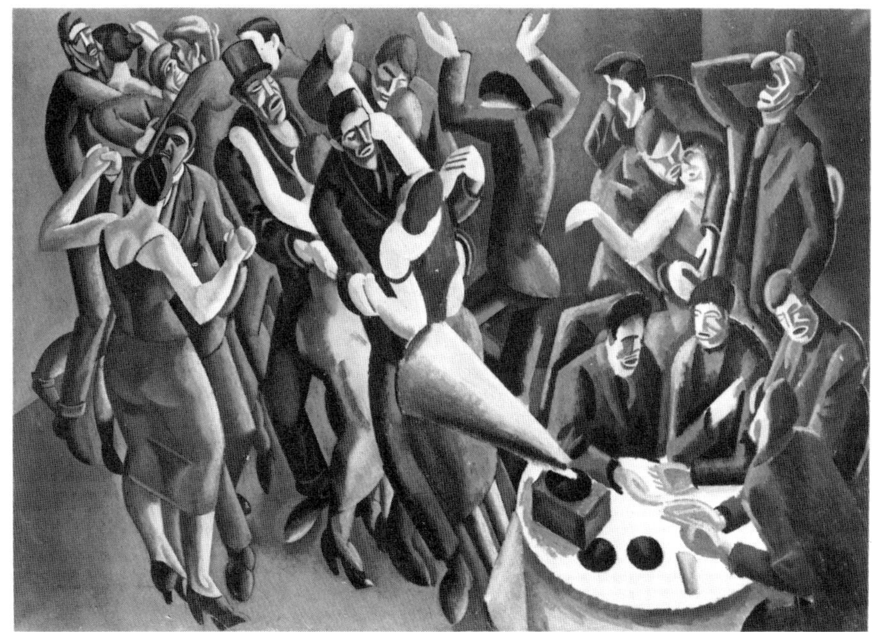

21 **Matthew Smith** 1879–1959
Lilies c. 1913
oil on canvas 30¼ × 22 in (76·8 × 55·9 cm)
signed

Matthew Smith spent most of his time
between 1910 and 1914 in France and his
painting of this period was much influenced
by Matisse in whose school he studied,
though only for a very short time. In sheer
brilliance of colour his work went beyond any
other by an English painter at this time. *Lilies*
was his first picture to be exhibited–at
Epstein's suggestion–at the London Group
in 1916.

Bought 1939

22 **Matthew Smith** 1879–1959
The Little Seamstress c. 1917
oil on canvas 36½ × 26 in (92·7 × 66 cm)
signed

In 1919 Matthew Smith was demobilised
from the army and could take up painting full
time again. This painting with its definite
outlines and rather fierce colour follows on
from the 'Fitzroy Street' nudes–his most
remarkable paintings during the war period.
This picture may have been painted before his
return to England from France.

Bought 1940

23 **William Roberts** 1895–1980
The Dance Club 1923
oil on canvas 30 × 42 in (76·2 × 106·6 cm)
signed

William Roberts had been associated with the
Vorticists in the years around 1914 but like
several other artists, after the war was over,
his interest in any kind of modernism gave
way to his own independent outlook. In
Roberts' case this was a profound interest in
people, at work, at home, at play. *The Dance
Club* is an early example of this abiding
concern, in which a Cubist influence–in the
facial types, the pattern-like composition–can
still be seen.

Given by the Contemporary Art Society, 1928

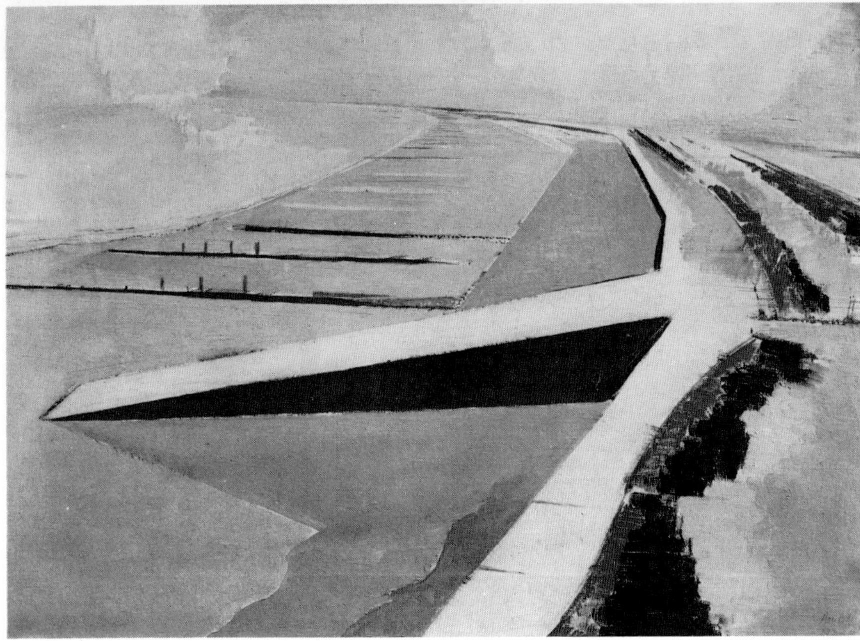

24 **Paul Nash** 1889–1946
The Shore 1923
oil on canvas $24\frac{1}{2} \times 37$ in $(62 \cdot 2 \times 94\,\text{cm})$
signed and dated

After the violence of Paul Nash's war
landscapes a certain element of threat
remained in the landscapes he painted at
Dymchurch in Kent where he and his wife
stayed from 1919 until 1925. They generally
show the sea wall holding back an angry
sea – *The Shore* is unusually serene, its calm
conveyed by a tendency to a simplified
abstraction which became more frequent in
Nash's work of the twenties.

Bought 1946

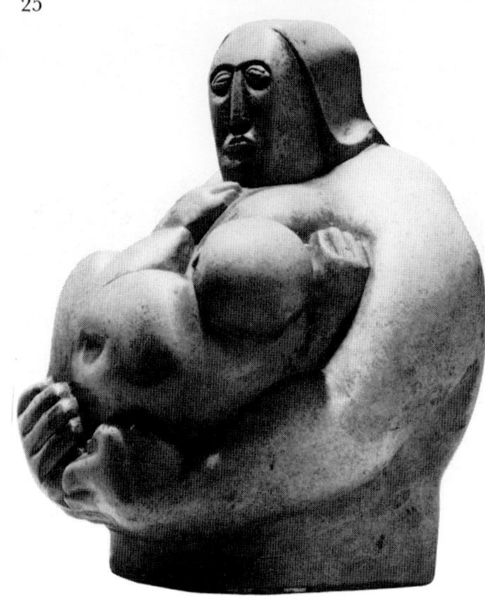

25 **Henry Moore** born 1898
Maternity 1924
Hoptonwood Stone h. $7\frac{7}{8}$ in $(27\,\text{cm})$

1924, when this carving was made, was Henry
Moore's last year at the Royal College of Art;
he then spent several months in Italy on a
travelling scholarship, returning to the
appointment offered him by the Principal, Sir
William Rothenstein, as sculptor instructor at
the College. This small mother and child
group is one of the sculptor's most powerful
early works. Its block-like solidity lacks the
flow and rhythm of later works but shows
already (apart from the obvious and much
written-about influences – African sculpture
and Post Impressionist art) the sculptor's
belief in his own way of seeing, and in the
value of direct carving and the way it could
express human feeling of the most
fundamental and important kind through the
use of very basic shapes.

Given by the Contemporary Art Society, 1946

26

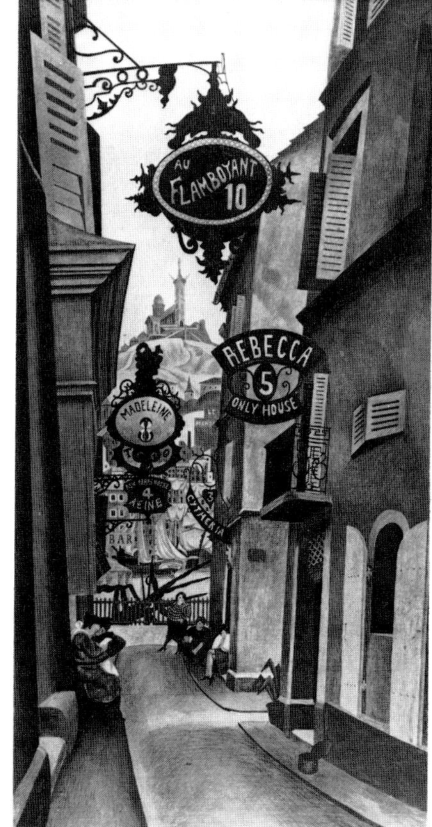

27

28

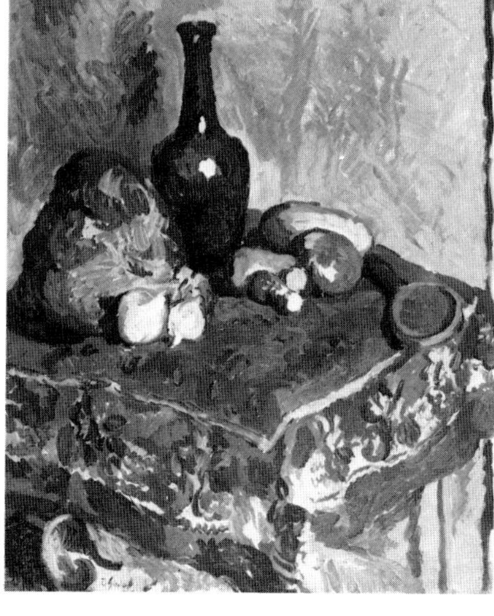

26 William Nicholson 1872–1949
On the Downs, Wiltshire 1924
oil on canvas $23\frac{1}{2} \times 21$ in (59·8 × 53·2 cm)
signed and dated

For about 10 years from 1923, the artist lived
at the Manor House at Sutton Veny in
Wiltshire, with his second wife Edith Stuart
Wortley whose father had bought them the
house as a present–from this period date a
whole series of landscapes of the Wiltshire
countryside.

*Bequeathed by H.M. Hepworth (Deputy Chairman
of the Art Gallery Sub-Committee from 1931 until
his death, and Treasurer of the* L.A.C.F.*), 1943*

27 Edward Wadsworth 1889–1949
Rue de la Reynarde, Marseille 1925
tempera on panel $37\frac{1}{2} \times 20$ in (95·2 × 50·8 cm)
signed and dated

Edward Wadsworth had been among
Wyndham Lewis's most radical associates
during the Vorticist and World War periods.
Immediately after the war he had worked on a
number of industrial subjects including those
for Michael Sadler's abortive project for the
decorations of Leeds Town Hall. Leeds owns
a number of his paintings from the 1920's
onwards, of which *Rue de la Reynarde* is the
earliest and most entertaining–like others of
Wadsworth's paintings of Marseilles it is
predominantly realistic with a hint of satire.

Bought 1943

28 Duncan Grant 1885–1978
Still Life 1930
oil on canvas 24×20 in (60·9 × 50·8 cm)
signed and dated

Duncan Grant's return about 1920 to a more
traditional rendering of solid forms,
compared to the bold experimentation of his
previous work, can be matched in the work of
other English painters of this period. It seems
to have been a particularly British reaction to
the return of peace. This still-life shows an
exuberance and love of rich colours which is
characteristic of the artist.

Bought 1931

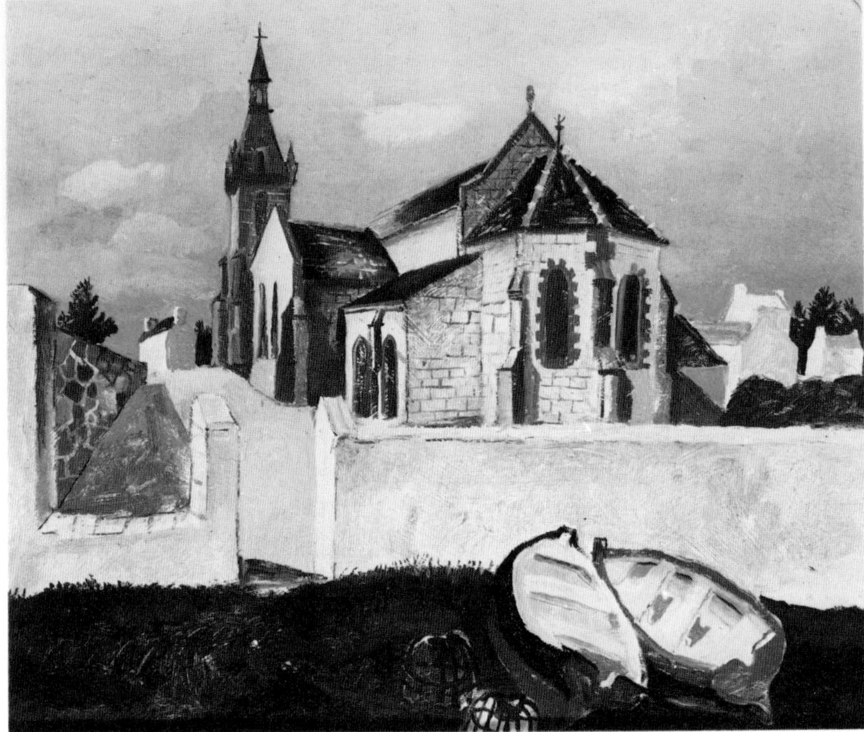

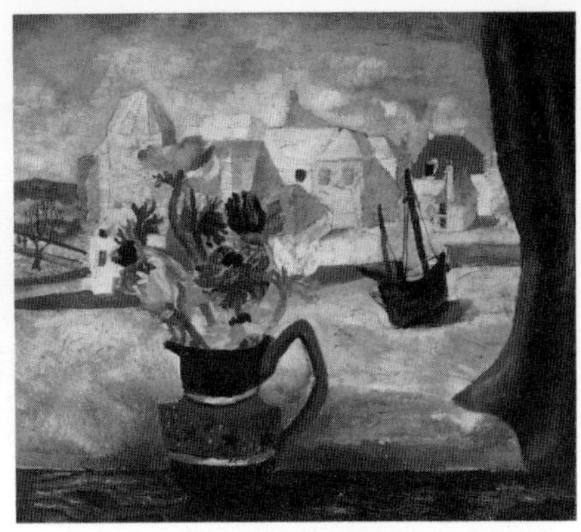

29 Christopher Wood 1901–1930
Treboul Church, Brittany 1930
oil on canvas 21 × 25¼ in (63·2 × 64 cm)
signed and dated

Painted during the last year of Wood's life, this is an example of Wood's liking for the landscape of the Breton coast, which has much in common with Cornwall, and which, like that area, had been a favourite summer painting place for artists since the 1890's. Christopher Wood visited Treboul first in 1929, returning in June of the following year, only two months before his early death.

Bought 1935

30 Christopher Wood 1901–1930
Anemones in a Cornish Window 1930
oil on canvas 16 × 19 in (40·6 × 48·2 cm)

Presumably painted on Christopher Wood's last visit to Cornwall the year he died. It was on a visit to St Ives in the summer of 1928 that he and Ben Nicholson had first met Alfred Wallis the retired fisherman turned painter, whose work encouraged Wood in his own fresh vision of the Cornish landscape.

Bought 1938

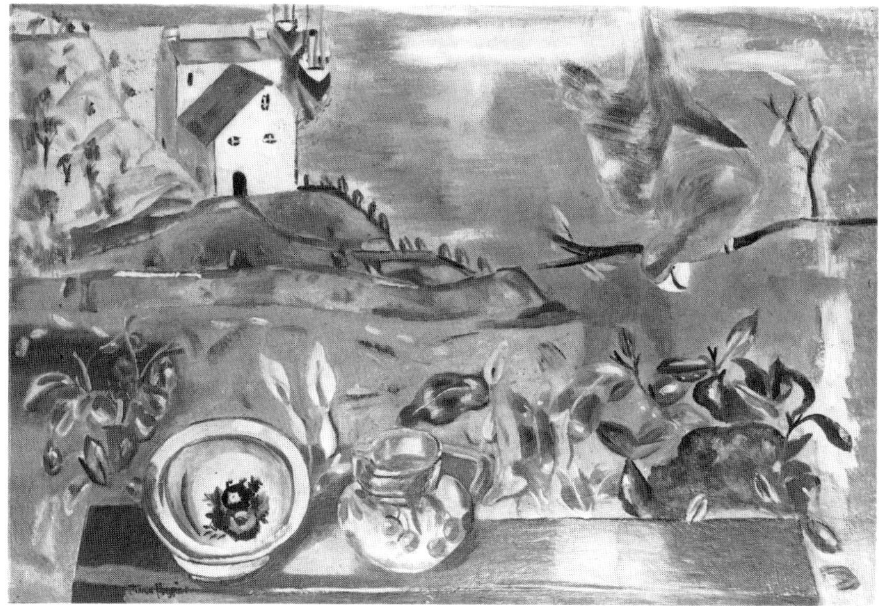

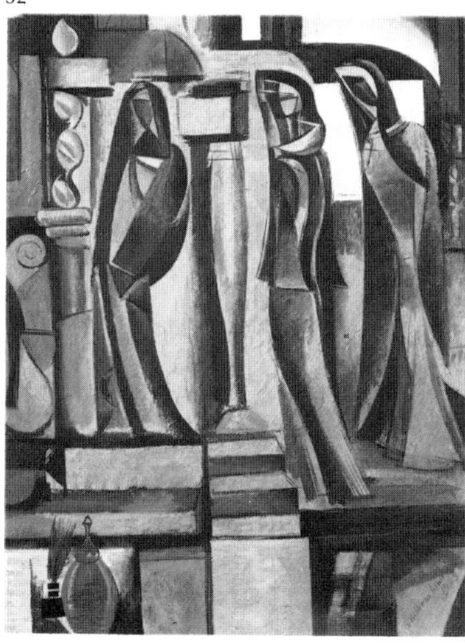

31 **Frances Hodgkins** 1869–1947
Wings over Water c. 1931–2
oil on canvas 27 × 38 in (68·6 × 96·5 cm)
signed

Although Frances Hodgkins is chiefly
remembered now for her original and poetic
paintings of the 1930's she was actually only
nine years younger than Sickert – her 'delayed
success' as she called it came after many years
of struggle, entailing the decision to leave her
native New Zealand at the age of 32 to
explore Europe and discover for herself 'the
masterpieces of all time'. After extensive
travel and several visits home, she settled in
England in 1914, still often visiting France.
She was elected to the Seven and Five Society
in 1929. *Wings over Water* was probably
painted at Bodinnick, Cornwall, in the winter
and spring of 1931–2.

Given by the Contemporary Art Society, 1940

32 **Wyndham Lewis** 1882–1957
Three Veiled Figures 1933
oil on canvas 21 × 17 in (53·5 × 43 cm)
signed and dated

During the 1920's Wyndham Lewis had
concentrated on writing and also on making
portrait drawings, but in 1932 he again
undertook a series of oil paintings. Despite
serious illness and two operations he had
completed ten of these by the following year.
These paintings were smaller in scale and
more delicately coloured than previous works
in oil and peopled with strange dream-like
beings drawn in a stylised manner,
reminiscent of Cubism but having little to do
with the theories of that movement. Rather it
enabled Lewis to give a kind of universality to
his images. These mysterious figures, whose
identity is unknown, seem to represent a
statue in a temple and two attendant
worshippers.

Bought 1978

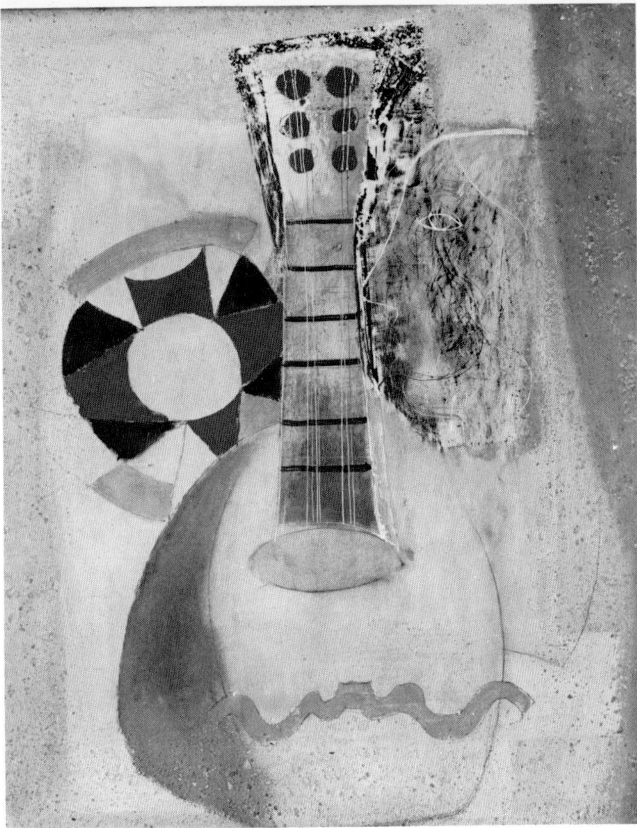

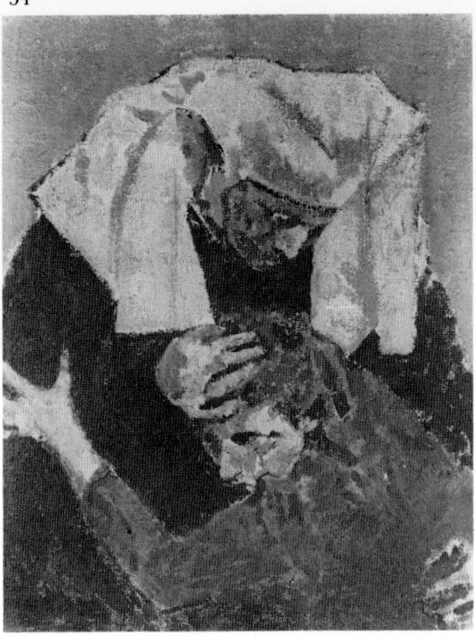

33 Ben Nicholson born 1894
Still Life with Guitar 1933
oil on board 30 × 25 in (76·2 × 63·5 cm)

This is one of several paintings of this period in which Ben Nicholson incised the drawing into a board prepared with special plaster, thus giving an object-quality to the painting and anticipating the white reliefs which he began to make this very year. (The reliefs were to be wholly abstract however.) *Still Life with Guitar* retains the imagery Nicholson had favoured for several years—the girl's profile is that of the sculptor Barbara Hepworth, with whom he had been working since 1932 and whom he was to marry.

Given by the Contemporary Art Society, 1950

34 Walter Richard Sickert 1860–1942
Juliet and the Nurse 1935–6
oil on canvas 30 × 24 in (76·2 × 60·9 cm)
signed

During the 1930's Sickert, who had always been attracted to the theatre, frequently attended performances, made friends with the actors and made paintings on their subjects. The paintings were usually derived from press photographs, and Edith Evans—here as the nurse—features in at least one other painting, and Peggy Ashcroft—here as Juliet—in several others.

The technique of painting from photographs (or other graphic sources, such as Victorian prints) was widely used by Sickert in the thirties—it encouraged a tonal (as opposed to linear) vision and Sickert used—or had his assistants use—a dry, 'scraped' brushwork, showing often bare canvas between paint areas, with a concentration on large masses curiously flattened—unparalleled before Andy Warhol.

Bought by the Leeds Art Collections Fund, 1937

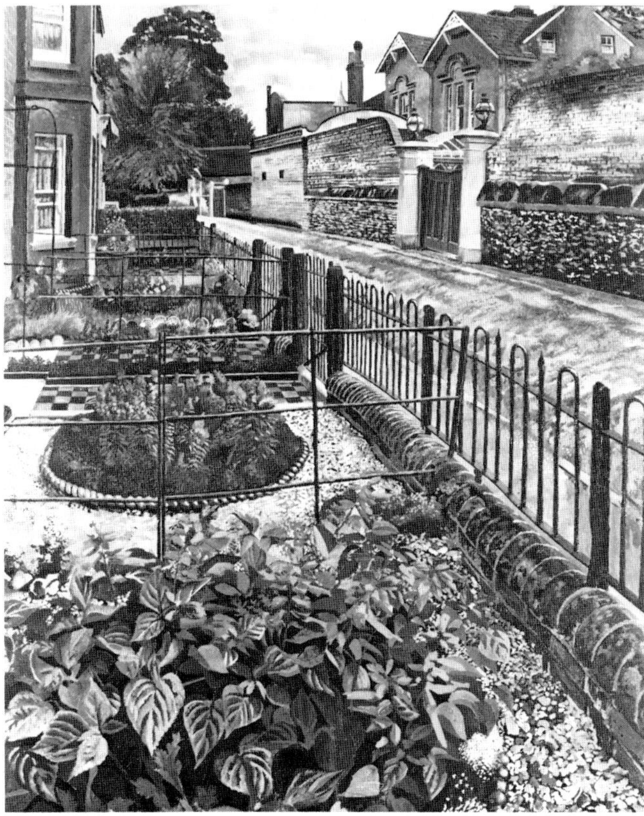

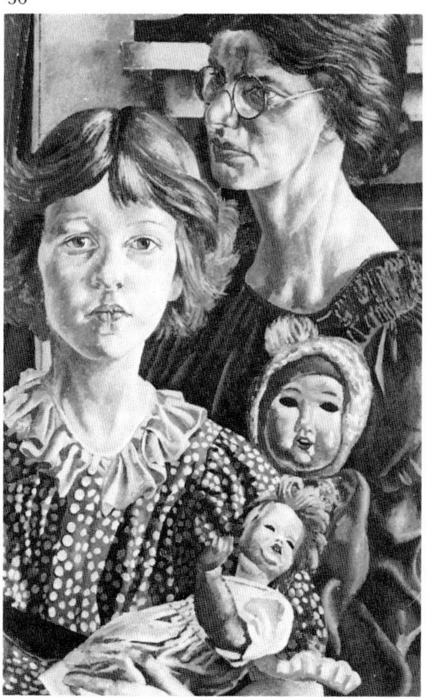

36 **Stanley Spencer** 1891–1959
Hilda, Unity and Dolls 1937
oil on canvas 30 × 20 in (76·2 × 50·8 cm)

35 **Stanley Spencer** 1891–1959
Gardens in the Pound, Cookham 1936
oil on canvas 36 × 30 in (91·4 × 76·2 cm)

Stanley Spencer's love for the village on the Thames where he grew up was legendary–during his years at the Slade (1908–12) he was nicknamed 'Cookham' by his fellow students. Although he complained that he had to paint too many landscapes, as they sold better than his more personal works, this boredom is not often betrayed in the actual pictures. Humble back-street gardens are delineated with a dedicated affection familiar from his paintings of people–the conventions of 'picturesque' landscape totally ignored in favour of suburban edging tiles, bedding plants (lobelia, salvias) and little iron railings.

Bought by the Leeds Art Collections Fund, 1940

Hilda Carline was Stanley Spencer's first wife; Unity Spencer is their younger daughter, seven years old at the time this portrait was painted. This painting is one of the best-loved in the Leeds collection, and though Stanley Spencer is known to have put a higher premium on his own more personal religious/allegorical paintings than on commissioned portraits and landscapes, in pictures of people close to him one can be sure he put of his very best. As in many of his paintings of domestic life his affection for the people concerned is seen in faithful characterisation, and in his delight in the actual texture and colours of such things as dress fabrics, a love for and fascination with the stuff of everyday life.

Bought 1938

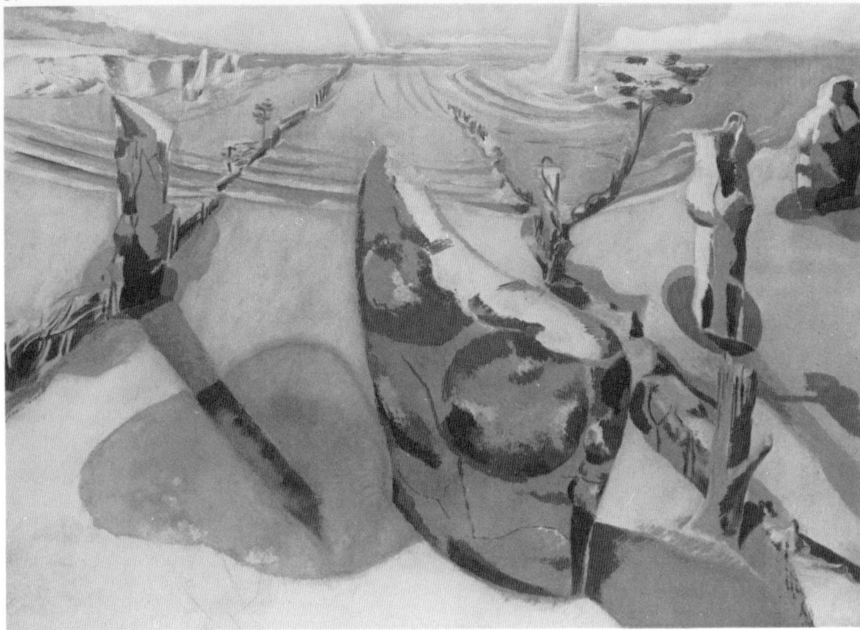

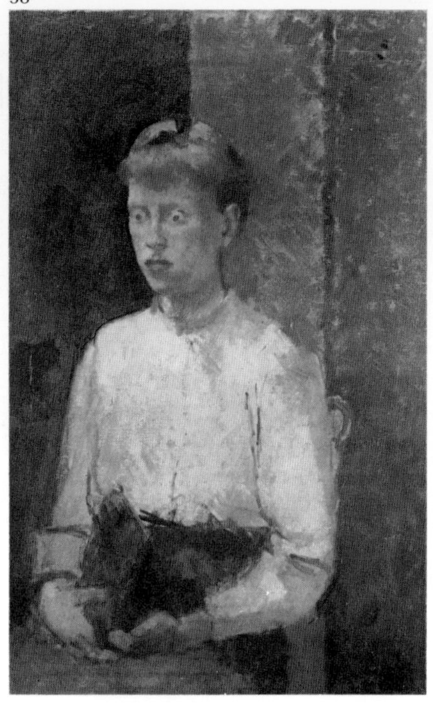

37 **Paul Nash** 1889–1946
Circle of the Monoliths 1937–8
oil on canvas 31 × 41 in (78·8 × 104·1 cm)
signed

There were two sides to Paul Nash's
imagination–the attractions both of 'modern
design', a tendency to abstraction which
found expression in paintings like *The Shore*
(and more completely in his work as a
designer) and his strong feeling for the
numinousness of particular places–present
from his earliest years, but seeming to find an
encouragement in the work of the Surrealist
artists whom he met in Paris with their stress
on the importance of dream-imagery. Of
course many people who are not artists have
felt strange sensations of communication
with past ages in the presence of prehistoric
monuments, but Nash was particularly able to
fix these sensations in paint. The components
of *Circle of the Monoliths* are the standing
stones at Avebury and the seashore and cliffs
at Swanage in Dorset–their juxtaposition was
described by Nash as 'a kind of dream'
concerned with 'two landscapes . . . with
whose appearance I was intimate, even
enchanted'.

Bought 1950

38 **Victor Pasmore** born 1908
Girl with a Handbag 1938
oil on canvas 30 × 20 in (76·2 × 50·8 cm)

The Euston Road School, opened by William
Coldstream, Victor Pasmore and Claude
Rogers from 1937 till the outbreak of war,
was a private school for drawing and
painting, where instruction was given in
working directly and realistically from the
live model; it was an attempt to provide a
positive alternative to the abstract and
surrealistic experiments current in the art
world at the time. Pasmore often painted
from the model alongside the students–this
painting is an example; it was bought by Sir
Kenneth Clark, a helpful patron to Pasmore at
this time.

Given by the Contemporary Art Society, 1946

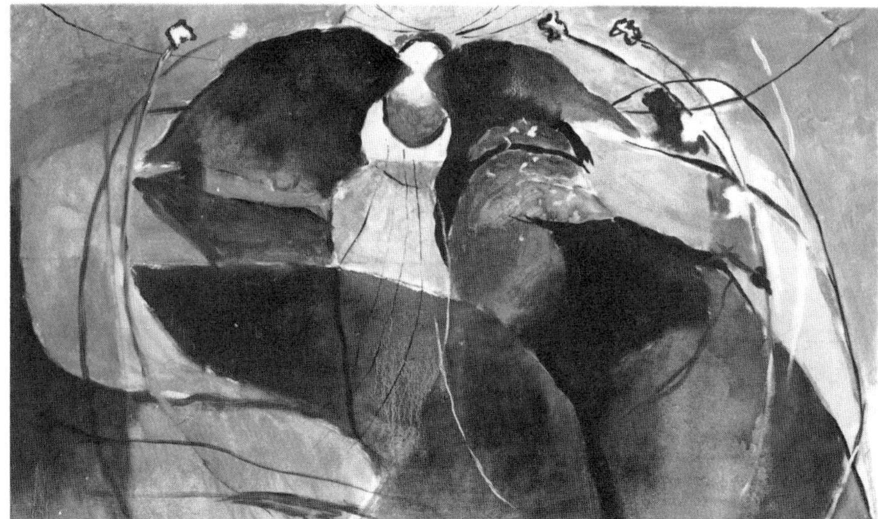

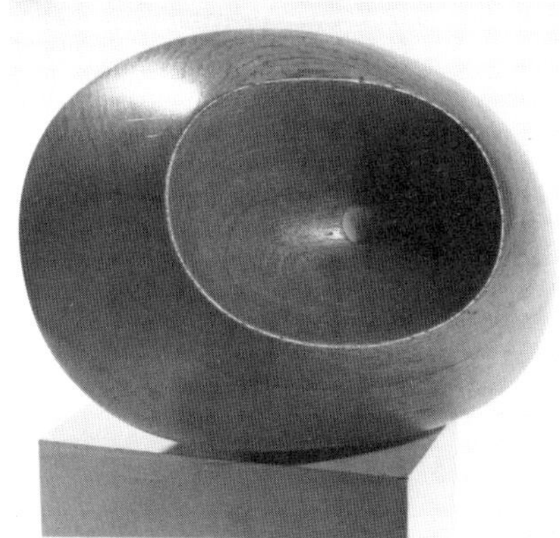

39 Graham Sutherland 1903–1980
Sunrise between Hedges 1939
oil on canvas $21\frac{1}{2} \times 35\frac{1}{2}$ in ($54 \cdot 6 \times 90 \cdot 2$ cm)

Bought for Leeds in 1941, two years after it was painted, this work no doubt appeared radically abstract at the time. Now it recalls more readily the romanticism of the Samuel Palmer-like landscape etchings with which Sutherland first made his name as an artist. Sutherland's ability to animate the inanimate, to express emotion through subjects which—like landscape, or later, in the war paintings, machinery—are not themselves capable of *having* emotions, is apparent in his most abstracted work. After the Second World War landscape was a subject to which he would return, between forays into the world of portraiture, and of paintings of tropical plants and of animals.

Bought 1941

40 Barbara Hepworth 1903–1975
Conicoid 1939
teak wood h. 8 in (20.3 cm)

From about 1934 Barbara Hepworth's work—direct carvings from various kinds of wood and stone—took on a particular purity and austerity of form; she wrote in 1936 of the feeling these forms gave her: 'a constructive work is an embodiment of freedom itself'. However the forms of the work were not based on a rigid geometry but intuitively arrived at, and never without some felt relationship to natural forms—as witness for instance her descriptions of the landscape around St Ives in Cornwall, which she discovered about this time and where she was subsequently to live for the rest of her life.

Bought 1943

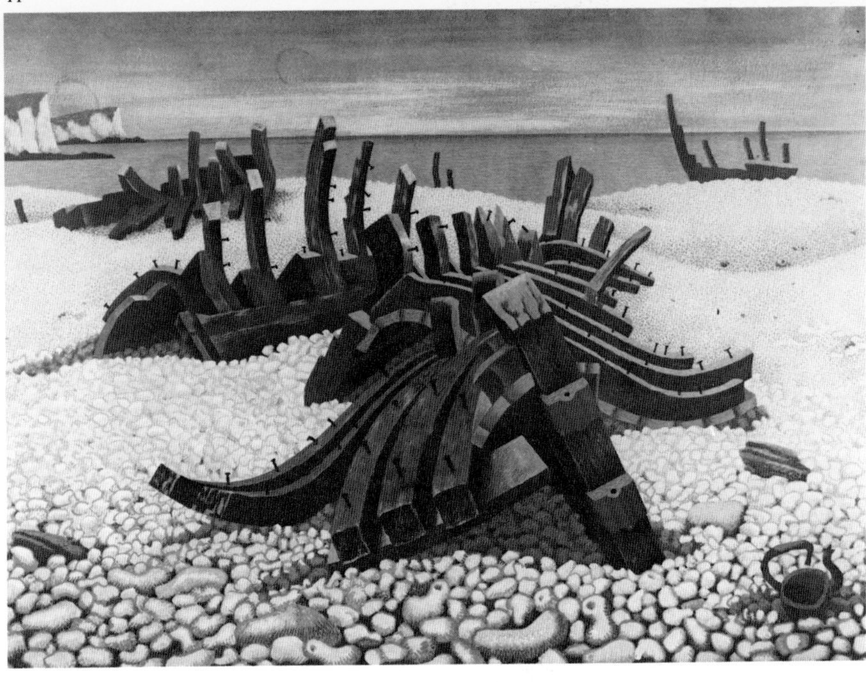

41 **Edward Wadsworth** 1889–1949
Requiescat 1940
tempera on panel 25 × 34 in (63·5 × 86·3 cm)

Paul Nash once wrote an article (in the
Architectural Review, 1936) on how to find
Surrealism in real life; this painting might
have been painted to illustrate how that piece
of writing might be taken literally.
'Requiescat in pace' – Rest in peace – from the
Latin Mass for the dead, is taken as a title for a
realistic (if simplified and stylised) depiction
of the skeletal timbers of a boat, left quietly to
rot on a deserted beach. Wadsworth shared
with Nash – whom he knew and had been
involved with in the short-lived 'Unit One'
group (founded by Nash in 1933 for the
promotion of new art) – an enthusiasm for
Surrealist ideas and a tendency to use them in
a very English way, taking images from the
real world and using them as if they had
occurred in a dream.

Bought 1941

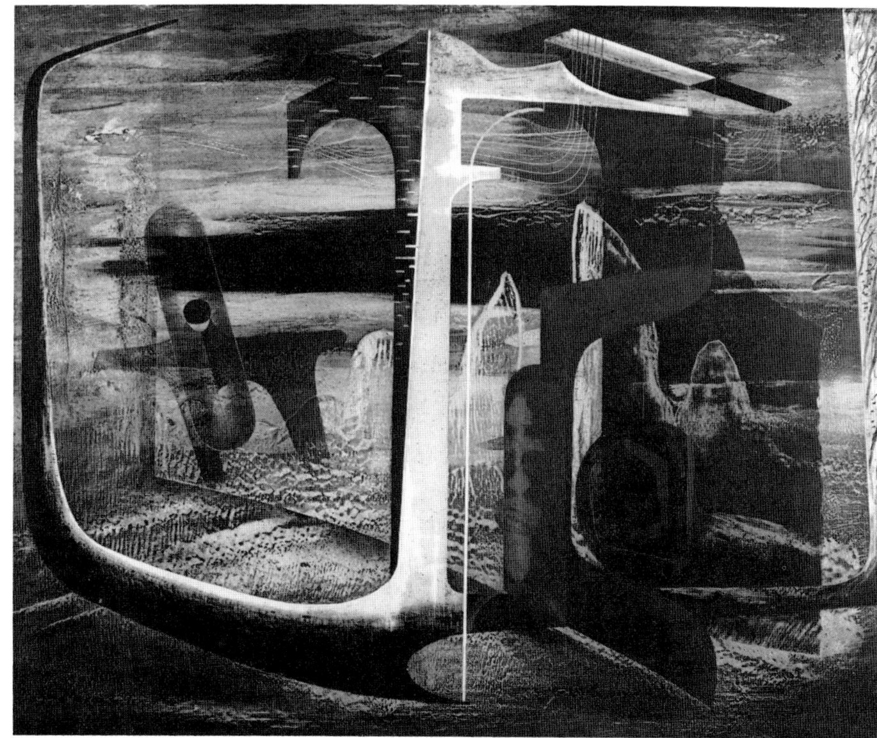

42 John Tunnard 1900–1971
Davy Jones's Locker 1940
oil on panel 20 × 25 in (50·8 × 63·5 cm)

The techniques of rubbing and scraping and graining of paint used in this work are those employed by the Surrealists (especially by Max Ernst), and the ghostly imagery – suggesting but not representing – ships' timbers, anchors, water-worn rocks, partakes clearly of the dream-like quality of surrealism.

'Davy Jones's Locker' is an old mariner's term for the sea – to 'go to Davy Jones's Locker' was to drown.

Bought by the Leeds Art Collections Fund, 1941

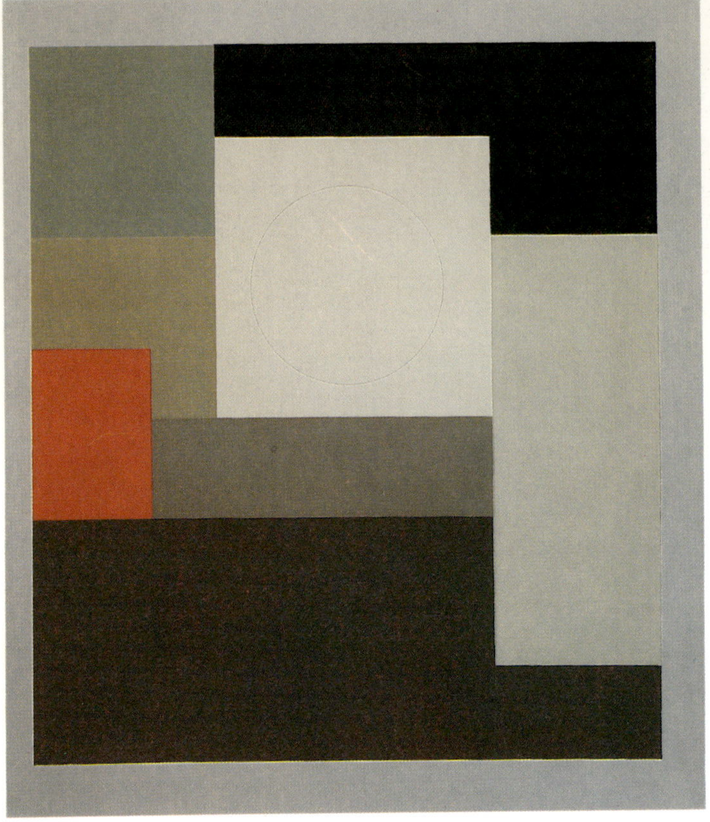

43 **Ben Nicholson** born 1894
Painting 1940
gouache on board 24 × 21 in (60·9 × 53·2 cm)
signed and dated

In 1944 an exhibition of work by Ben
Nicholson was held at Temple Newsam
House. It was one of a series of one- or two-
man exhibitions, which were regularly
arranged by Philip Hendy between 1935 and
1945, including virtually all British artists of
distinction at that time. A work was often
bought from the exhibition for the permanent
collection (it was in this manner that Henry
Moore's *Reclining Figure* of 1929 was
acquired). Reading between the lines in the
correspondence in the Gallery files it is
possible to sense a slight disappointment on
Ben Nicholson's part, that a grander work
had not been chosen – however, *Painting 1940*
must have been, as a work of totally
uncompromising abstraction, the most
'advanced' work to enter the collection at that
date.

Bought 1945

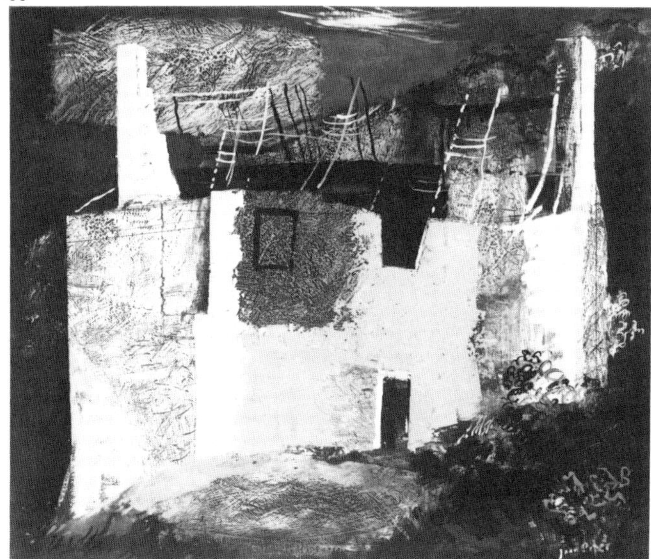

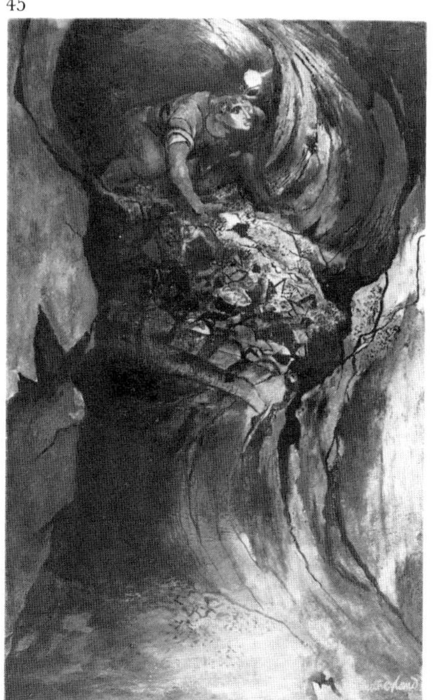

44 **John Piper** born 1903
Derelict Cottage, Llanthony 1941
oil on canvas 25 × 30 in (63·5 × 76·2 cm)
signed

Despite a clear relationship with Piper's pre-
war experiments with abstraction – the flat
planes and primary colours – this is a
landscape thoroughly in the British romantic
landscape tradition – the artist's sympathy
with this tradition is further demonstrated by
the publication, in the year following this
painting, of his book on *British Romantic
Artists* in the 'Britain in Pictures' series. Its
stormy, dramatic qualities are a reminder that
Piper has often been asked to design for the
stage, especially for opera and ballet.

Bought 1941

45 **Graham Sutherland** 1903–1980
Tin Mine : Emerging Miner 1944
gouache 46 × 28¾ in (116·8 × 73 cm)
signed

Graham Sutherland's work for the War
Artists' Committee is exceptional in his
oeuvre in containing a narrative element. He
drew and painted many studies of machinery
shattered by bombing, as a kind of metaphor
for wounded humanity ; he also made pictures
of the human effort at home, especially in the
mines, which constituted the backing for the
troops at the front. The strong 'landscape'
element in these pictures reminds us that for
miners work is always a battle, whether in
peace or war, against natural forces.

*Given by H.M. Government through the War
Artists' Advisory Committee, 1947*

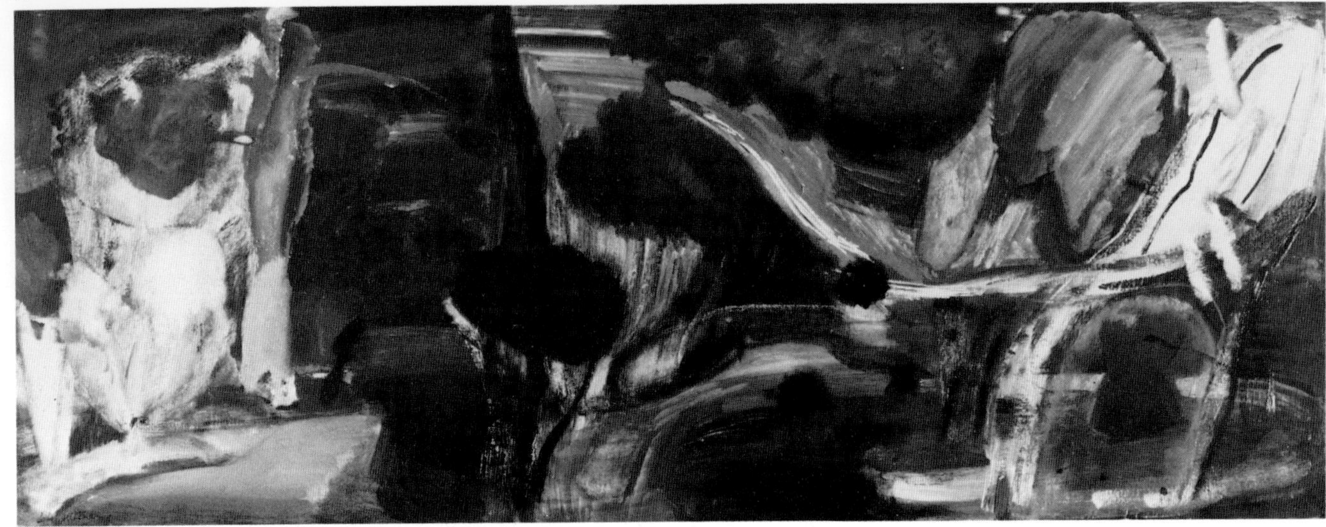

46 Ivon Hitchens born 1893
Hazel Wood 1944
oil on canvas 22 × 59 in (55·8 × 149·8 cm)
signed and dated

Hazel Wood, included in Ivon Hitchens'
exhibition at the Leicester Galleries in 1944,
was shown again at Temple Newsam the
following year in the exhibition which he
shared with Henry Moore and which was his
first retrospective show. He was beginning to
use with confidence the low wide format for
his characteristic landscapes, presenting a
sensitive re-interpretation of the natural
colours and spaces to be found in the Sussex
woodlands. These paintings hover on the
edge of abstraction – the artist has described
them as 'pictures painted to be listened to'.

Bought 1945

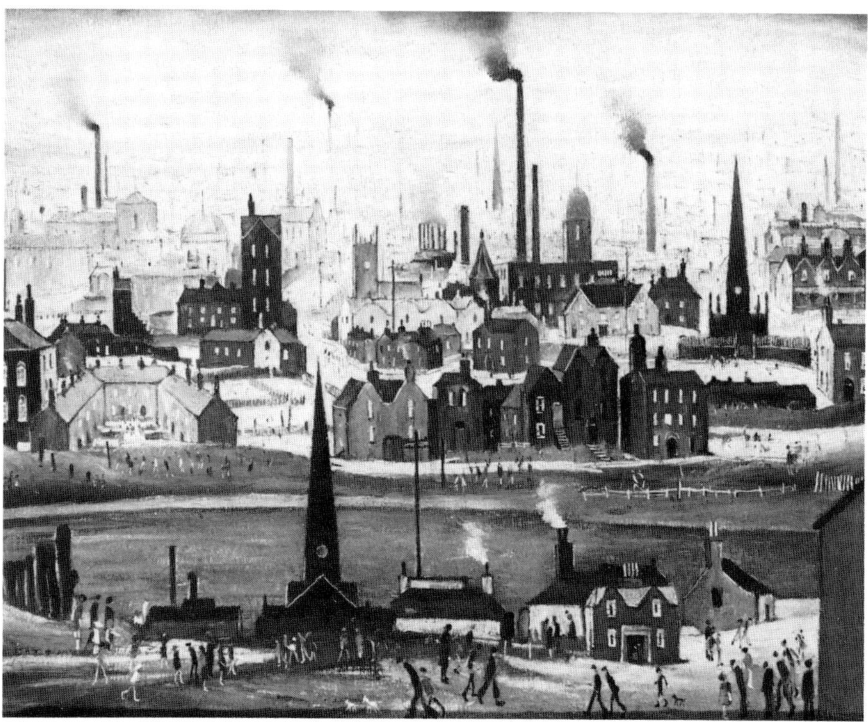

47 **L.S. Lowry** 1887–1976
The Canal 1945
oil on canvas 24 × 30 in (60·9 × 76·2 cm)
signed and dated

This painting is not a view of a specific place,
but rather one of Lowry's collations of many
buildings – mills, churches, streets with their
inhabitants, seen in a grey misty
atmosphere – which seemed to the artist to
typify the Salford area where he grew up and
spent his working life.

Given by the Leeds Art Collections Fund, 1948

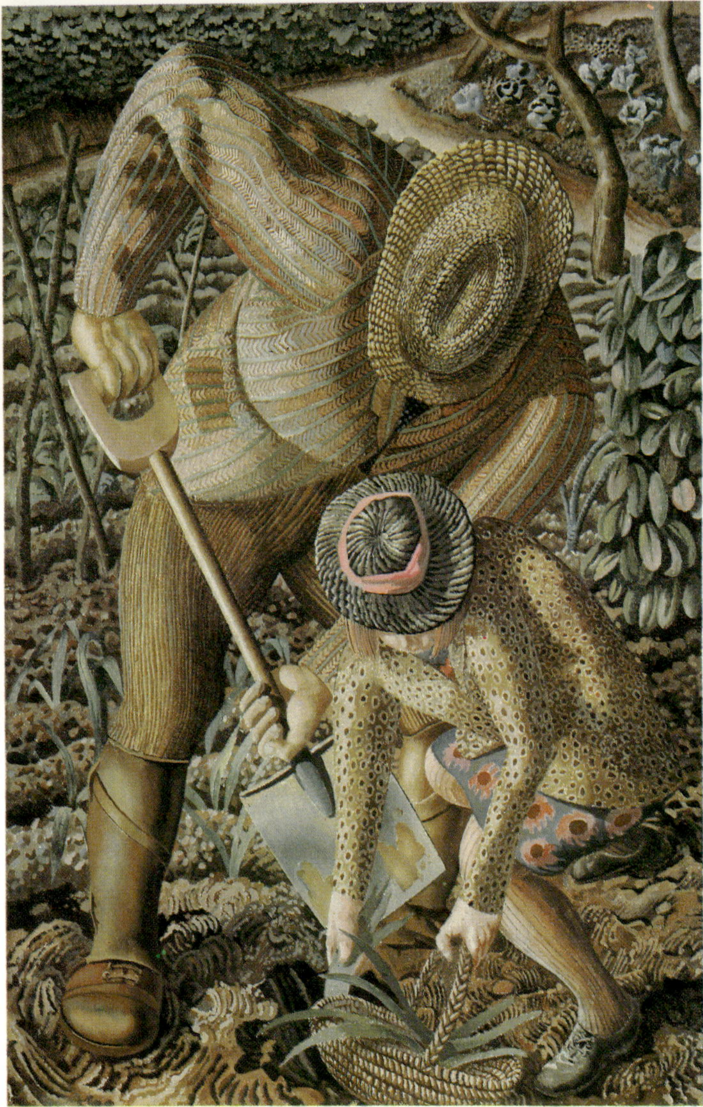

48 Stanley Spencer 1891–1959
Gardening 1945
oil on canvas 30 × 20 in (76·2 × 50·8 cm)

Stanley Spencer made the doings of everyday
domestic life a frequent subject treated with
what can only be called a kind of reverence.
This appears in *Gardening* not only in the care
with which he paints plant leaves, muddy
ground (stylised into little whorls and curls
like Leonardo waterfalls) the textures of
tweed jackets and cotton print frocks and the
weave of a basket, but also in the ease with
which, like the medieval artists he admired, he
paints the two figures on quite different scales
to fit them comfortably into the composition.

Bought 1950

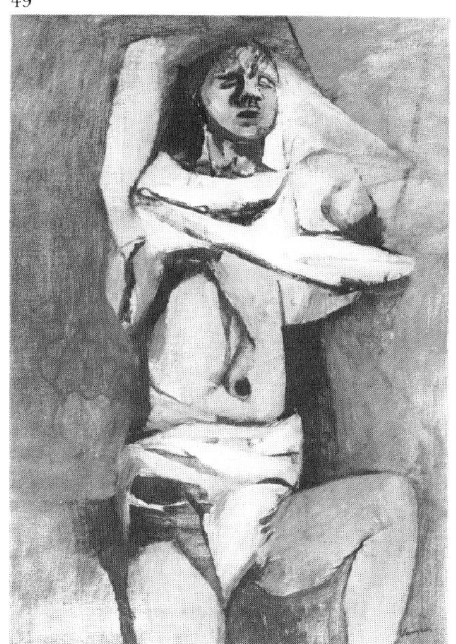

50 **Tristram Hillier** born 1905
Whitstable Oystermen 1948
oil on canvas 32 × 24 in (81·3 × 60·9 cm)
signed and dated

Whitstable is a town on the North Kent coast
famous for its oyster fishery. Ships and boats
are a favourite subject with this artist, who
spent some time in the summers before the
war sailing in the Mediterranean. Hillier's
precisely detailed rendering of the fishing
boats, their tackle and the shingled beach
creates an atmosphere of stillness almost
dreamlike in its intensity, hardly broken by
the flight of the seagull seen against the right-
hand boat.

Bought 1949

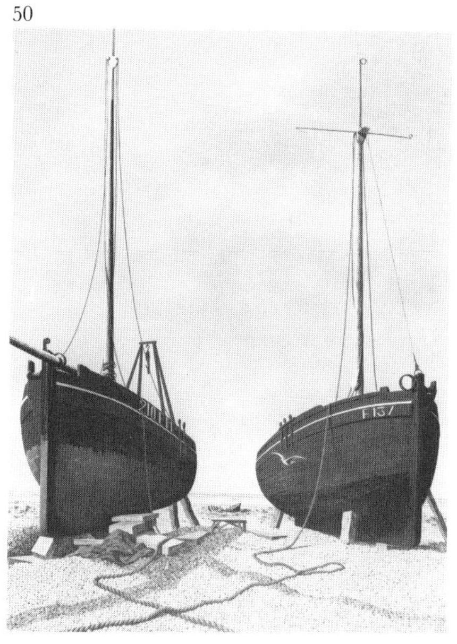

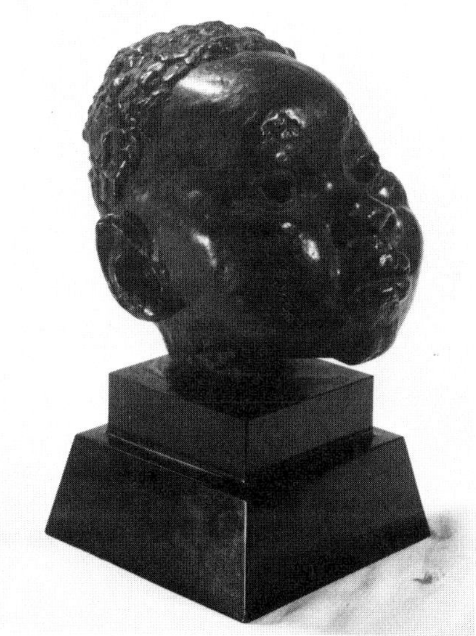

49 **Keith Vaughan** 1912–1979
Figure Undressing 1947
oil on canvas
22 × 16¼ in (56 × 41·2 cm)

At the time this picture was made Keith
Vaughan who, like many other artists of his
generation, had spent the war in the armed
forces with a consequent break of several
years from serious painting, was sharing a
studio with John Minton. He shared also with
him and others the label of 'neo-Romantic'
attached to their painting by critics. This
small figure study does indeed have a prickly,
anguished look to it not found in Vaughan's
later, more serene paintings of figures in
landscape.

Bought by the Leeds Art Collections Fund, 1951

51 **Jacob Epstein** 1880–1959
Victor 1949
Bronze h. 6¾ in (17·5 cm)

Epstein frequently chose children—his own
and other people's—as models, and his child
portraits are among his most expressive
works. Victor was the small son of the
Epsteins' West African cook, who came to
them in 1949.

*Bequeathed in 1973 by Jocelyn Horner to the Leeds
Art Collections Fund (in Memory of Ernest
Musgrave, Director of Leeds Art Galleries
1946–58)*

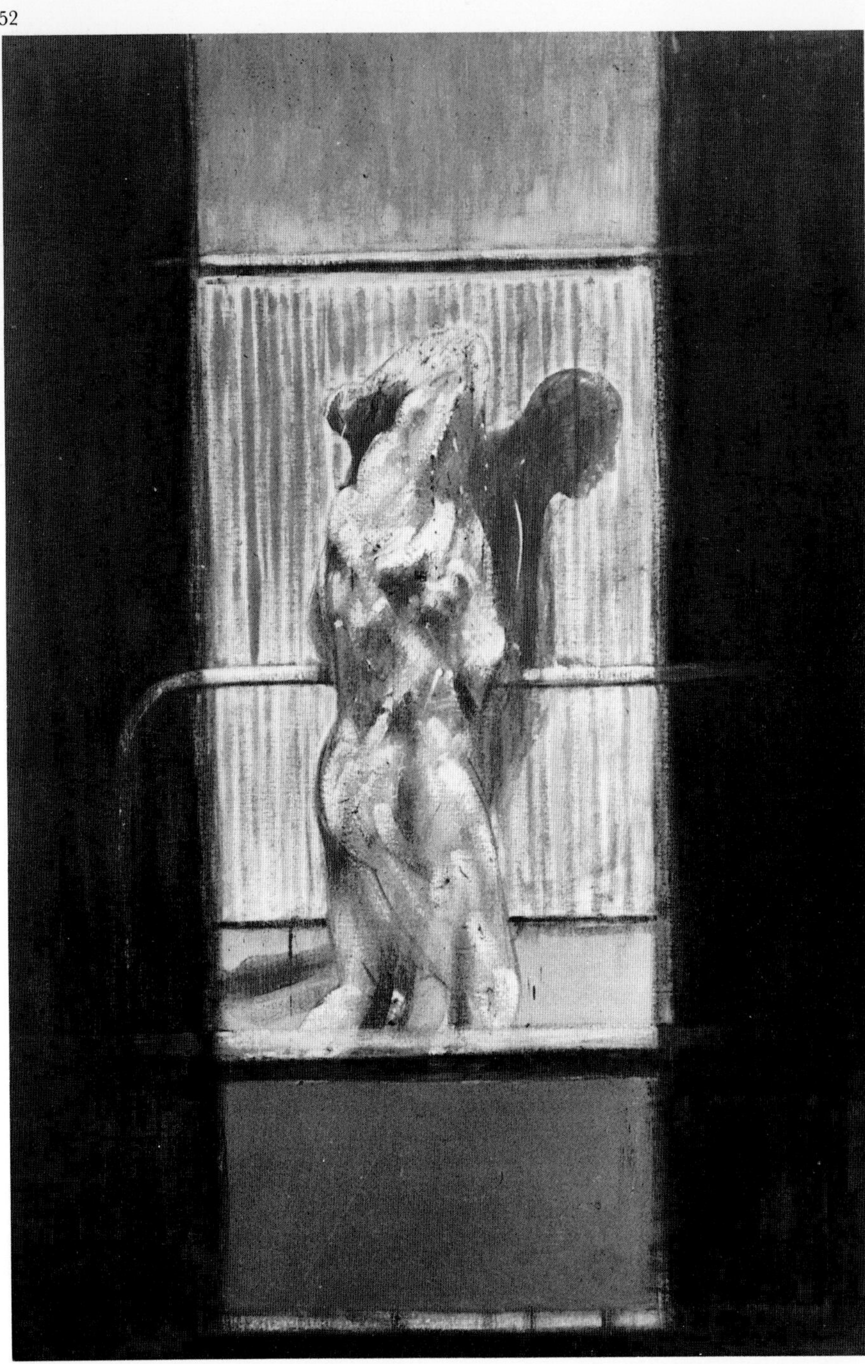

52 **Francis Bacon** born 1909
Painting 1950
oil on canvas 78 × 52 in (198 × 132 cm)

This painting is possibly one of the first in which the artist derived images from photographs by Eadweard Muybridge of the human figure in motion – these photographs of walking and running people are taken against a regular grid (for measurement purposes). Bacon has exploited – exaggerated, altered, added to, with intense emotional effect – both the grid and the figure. Its ambiguous placement in space and its surprising shadow (is it another figure?) gives this painting mysterious urgency (which contrasts with the public optimism of the Festival of Britain, the year in which the painting was bought for the Gallery).

Bought by the Leeds Art Collections Fund, 1951

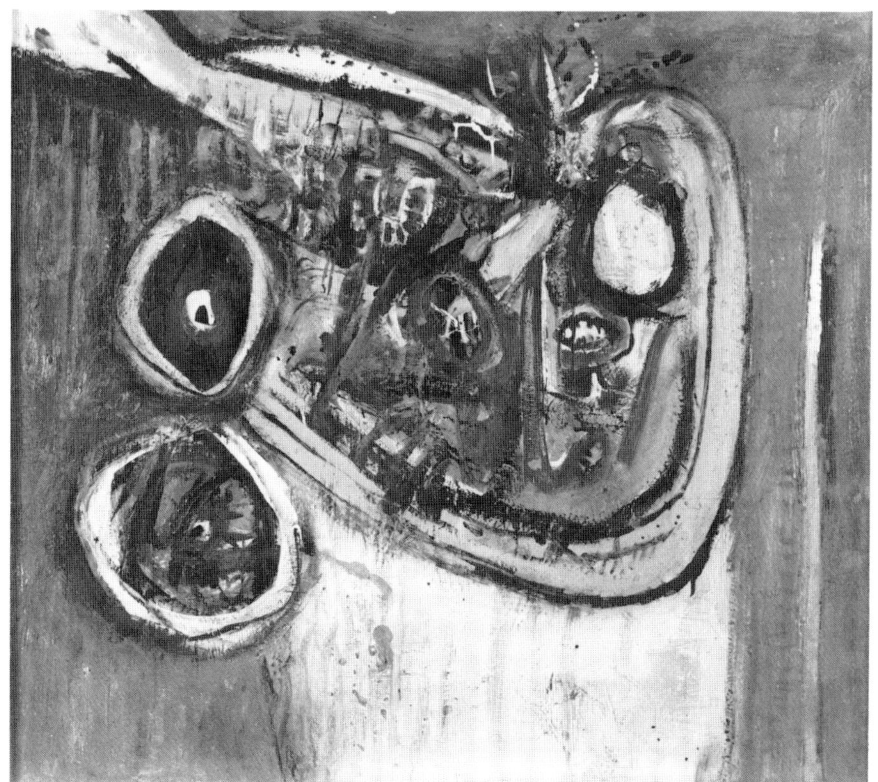

53 **Alan Davie** born 1920
In the Face of the Witch 1955
oil on board $39\frac{1}{4} \times 46$ in (99·7 × 116·8 cm)

Alan Davie's paintings of the mid-1950's
were sufficiently 'abstract' in their imagery
and free and expressionistic in their brush
work to be described at the time as 'action-
painting' as if they were British equivalents to
the works of Pollock (which Davie was one of
the first British artists to see) and Kline in
New York. In fact Davie's paintings work
rather differently; each painting often began
as an abstract sign and developed, during the
working process, complex and allusive, often
archaic or (as here) primitive imagery with
ambiguously magical or ritualistic
significance.

Given by the Contemporary Art Society, 1962

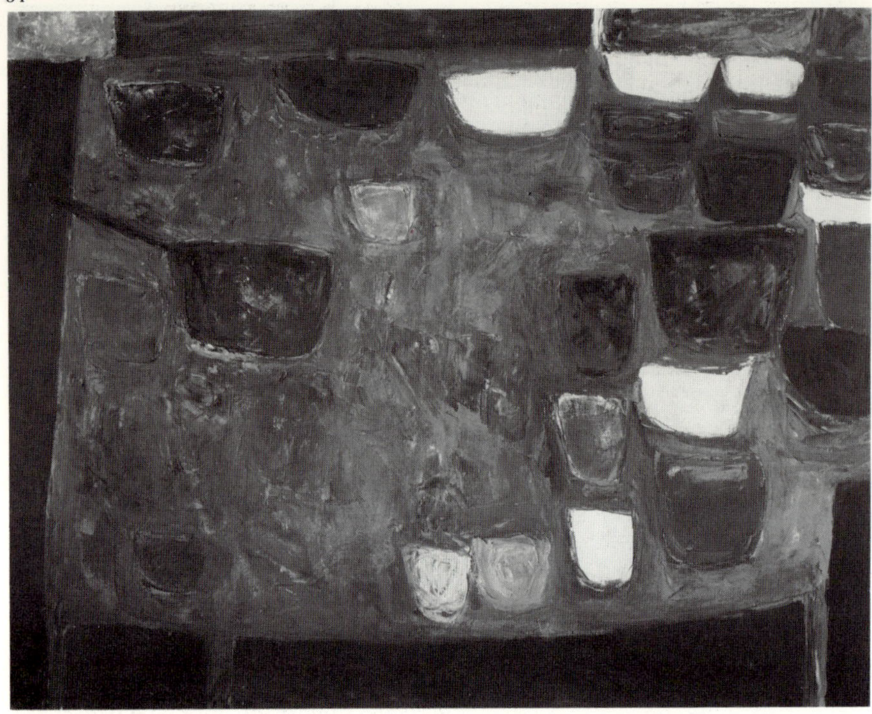

54 **William Scott** born 1913
Blue Still Life 1957
oil on canvas 42 × 52 in (106·6 × 132·1 cm)

William Scott's most abstract paintings are in
the classic European tradition. They are
abstractions from the motif, usually still-life,
characteristically bowls and saucepans,
simplified, spaced out, subjected to an overall
colour scheme which gives expressive mood
to each painting. In 1953 William Scott
visited the USA and became acquainted with
several of the leading artists in New York.
While remaining deeply admiring of their
work his own response was to return with
renewed conviction to his European
roots – his paintings of the later 1950's reveal
more clearly their still life origins than some
of his preceding works.

Given by the Contemporary Art Society, 1959

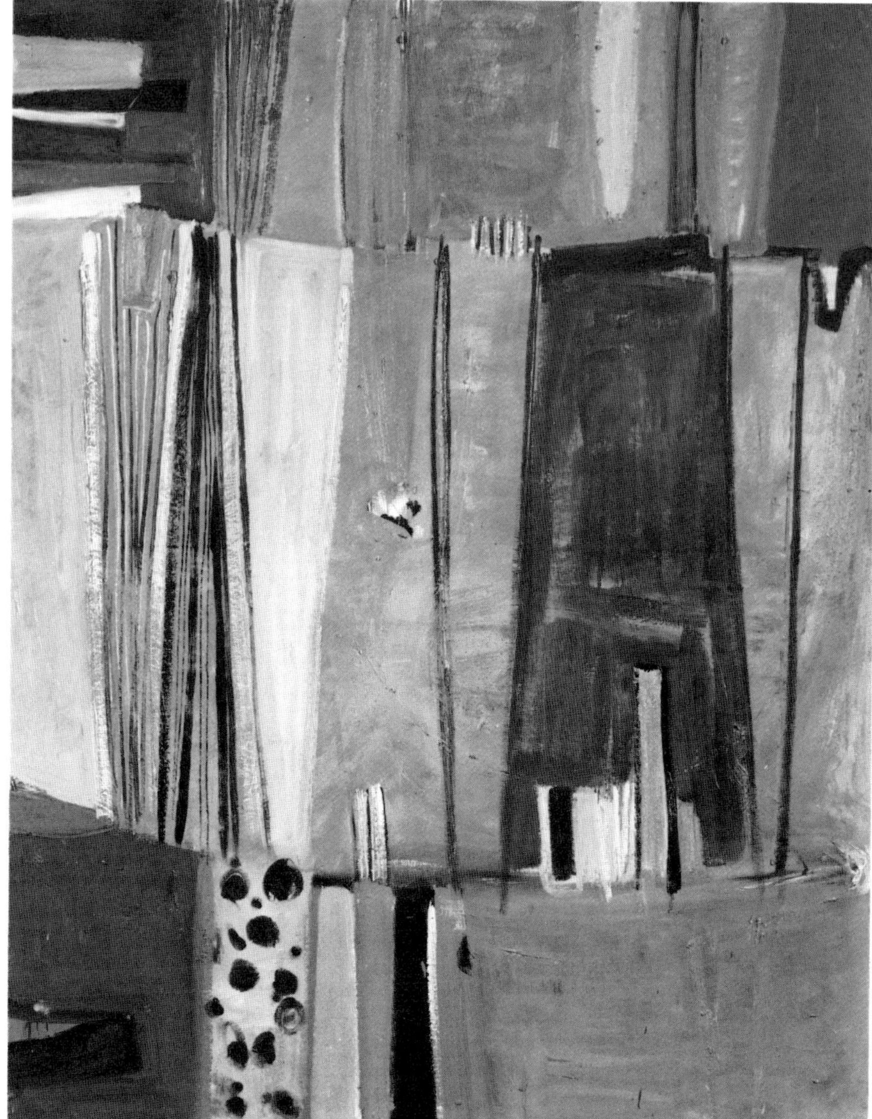

55 **Terry Frost** born 1915
Brown Verticals 1958–9
oil on canvas 78 × 68 in (213·4 × 172·7 cm)

Terry Frost has been making abstract
paintings, abstract in the sense that they do
not betray at first sight any connection with
recognisable objects, since 1949. They are
however often based upon experiences of
landscape, in the later fifties specifically the
Yorkshire landscape of bare hills and stone
walls, which made a deep impression on
Terry Frost when he moved to Leeds in 1954
for three years as Gregory Fellow in painting.
He would stress that it is the total feeling of
the landscape which is expressed in a work
which once begun, grows during the process
of painting by its own laws – the interaction of
colours and forms.

Bought by the Leeds Art Collections Fund, 1960

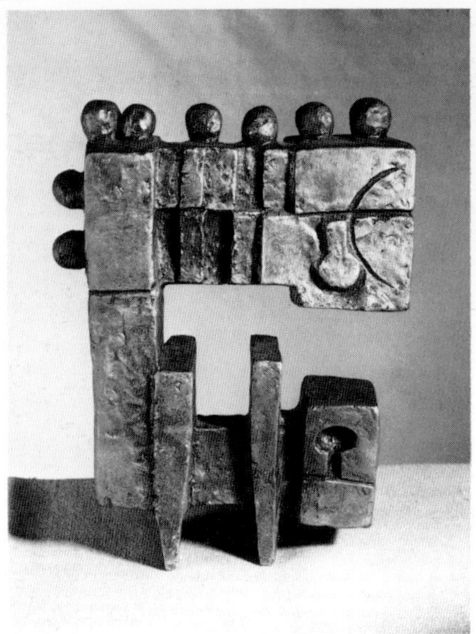

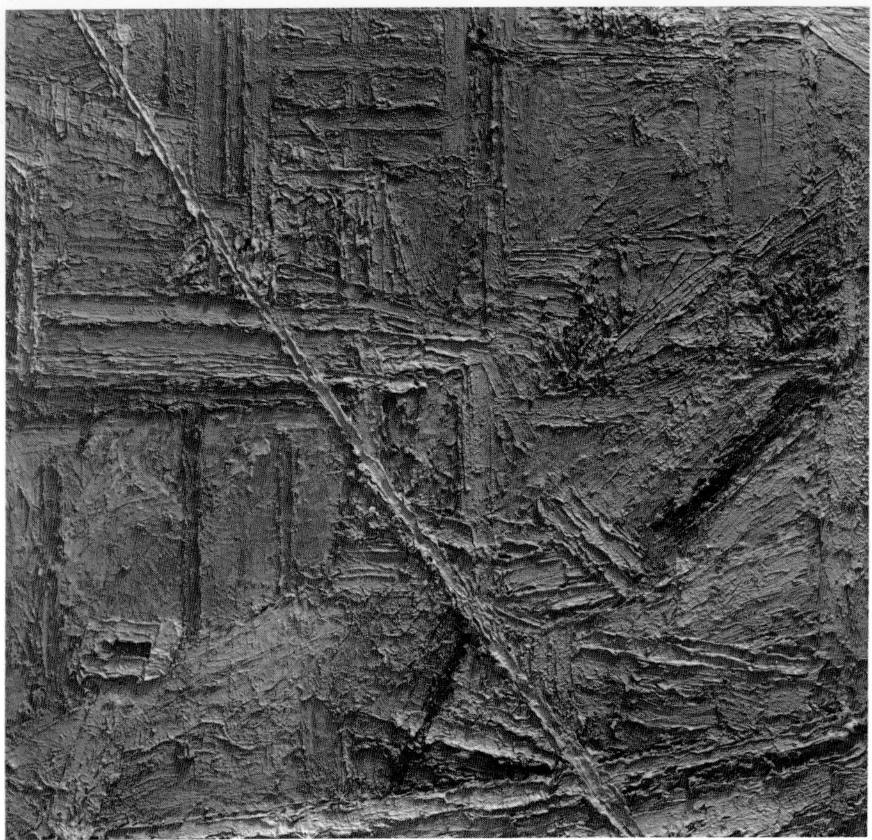

56 **Hubert Dalwood** 1924–1976
Object : Open Square 1959
aluminium h. 16½ in (42 cm)

Hubert Dalwood held the Gregory
Fellowship in Sculpture at Leeds University
1955–1958 (coinciding with first Terry Frost
and then Alan Davie as Fellows in Painting),
and continued for another six years as a
popular and influential teacher at Leeds
College of Art. *Open Square* is made in
aluminium (whose use as a sculptural medium
Dalwood was pioneering at this time). Both
abstract and familiar forms are combined in
this piece (the keyhole motif was a favourite at
this period – it is an everyday household
object but can carry symbolic overtones – of
locked secrets, opening doors and so on) – to
create a kind of ritual object for our own time.

*Given anonymously to the Leeds Art Collections
Fund, 1960*

57 **Frank Auerbach** born 1931
Maples Demolition, Euston Road, 1960
oil on board 58½ × 60½ in (148·5 × 153·7 cm)

A number of the landscapes by Frank
Auerbach in the fifties and early sixties were
of building sites. The sharp vertical,
horizontal and diagonal lines offered by piles
and scaffold poles seem to have offered an
alternative kind of structure to his more
frequent subject, the human figure. In the
working and reworking of the painting these
lines and the spaces they define have become
more important than actual description of
objects, which have lost definition under an
accretion of rich impasto.

Given by the Contemporary Art Society, 1965

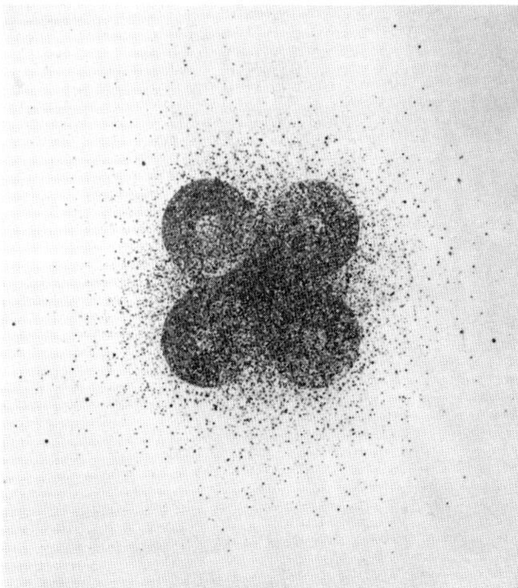

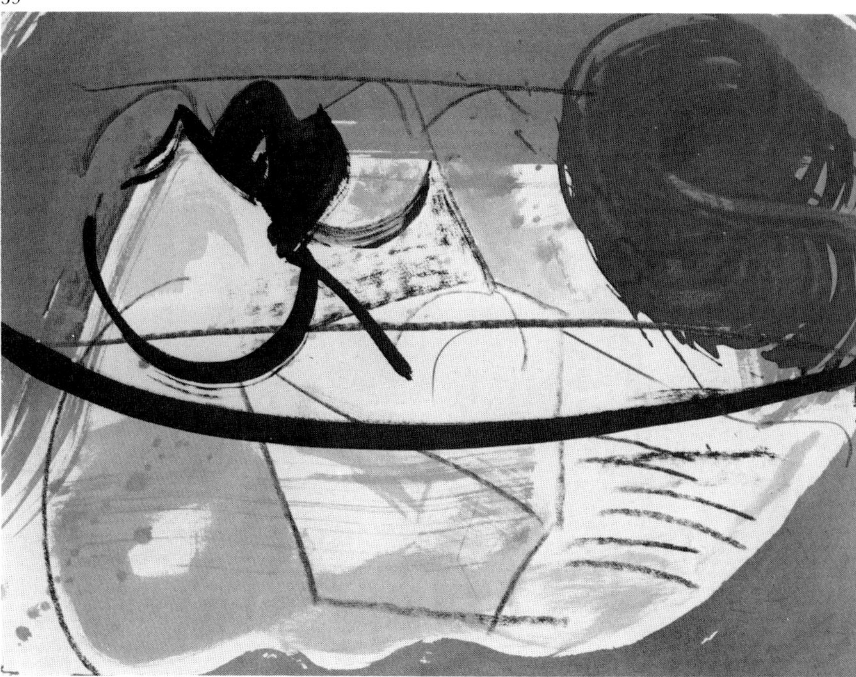

58 **Ian Stephenson** born 1934
Circumspect 2 (Spray Study) 1964
oil and collage on paper 24 × 22 in
(61 × 56 cm)

Ian Stephenson's small works on paper are
not to be seen as drawings – in the sense of
sketches, studies, less finished in any way than
his works on canvas. They are in fact small
paintings in their own right – but whereas
during this period the larger paintings
consisted usually of single all-over fields of
sprayed colour, the works on paper contained
incidents – collaged shapes like the four circles
in this example which act as a focus for the
atmospheric, evanescent colour in which they
seem to float. In these works – while the
spectator is never asked to believe that there is
anything there he can't actually see – each
drawing seems to open up the possibilities
suggested by light and colour and space.

Given by the Contemporary Art Society, 1979

59 **Peter Lanyon** 1918–1964
Clevedon Belle 1964
gouache on paper $22\frac{1}{2} \times 29\frac{7}{8}$ in (57×76 cm)

Clevedon is a seaside town near Bristol, where
Peter Lanyon took a party of students, in May
of the year he died, to look for landscape
subjects. He himself made a number of
drawings and photographs to be developed
into gouaches and oil paintings. Lanyon's
love of landscape (and his most 'abstract'
paintings were based on landscape forms) did
not exclude human elements – the *Clevedon
Belle* was one of the gaily painted pleasure
boats drawn up at the pier.

Bought by the Leeds Art Collections Fund, 1971

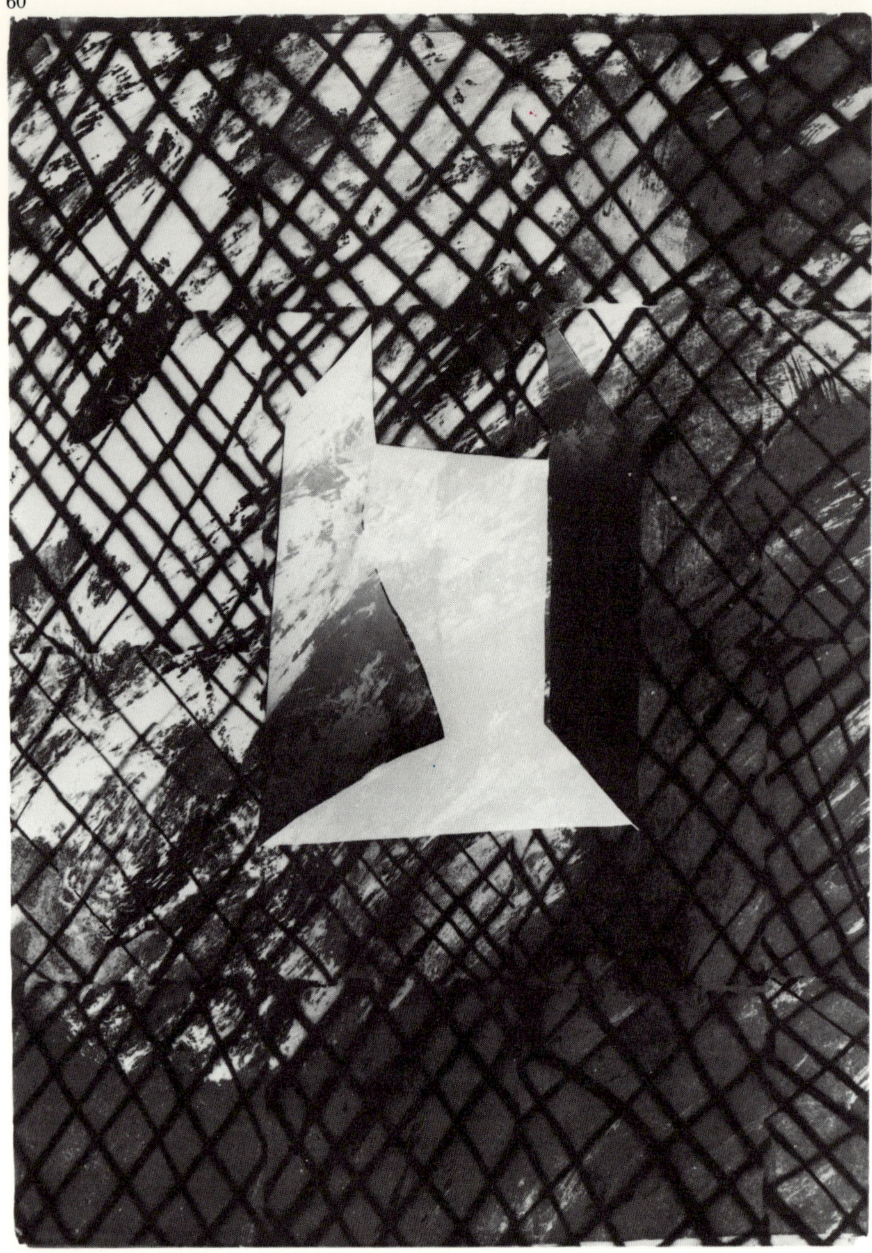

60 **John Walker** born 1939
Image No. 3 1965/1972
lithograph and screenprint $55\frac{1}{2} \times 40\frac{1}{2}$ in
($141 \times 102\cdot5$ cm)
signed and dated

In 1965 John Walker did a series of paintings
in which an irregular grid made a background
for a collaged shape—a shape not *quite*
recognisable as anything seen in the real
world—which was fixed on the canvas in a
position carefully calculated to seem both
floating free and at the same time tensely held
by the edges of the canvas. The resulting
paintings seemed charged with emotional
mystery. In the screenprints based on this
series, made seven years later, this was
enhanced by introducing textured effects in
both background and image, adding to the
ambiguities of space and subject.

Bought by the Leeds Art Collections Fund, 1973

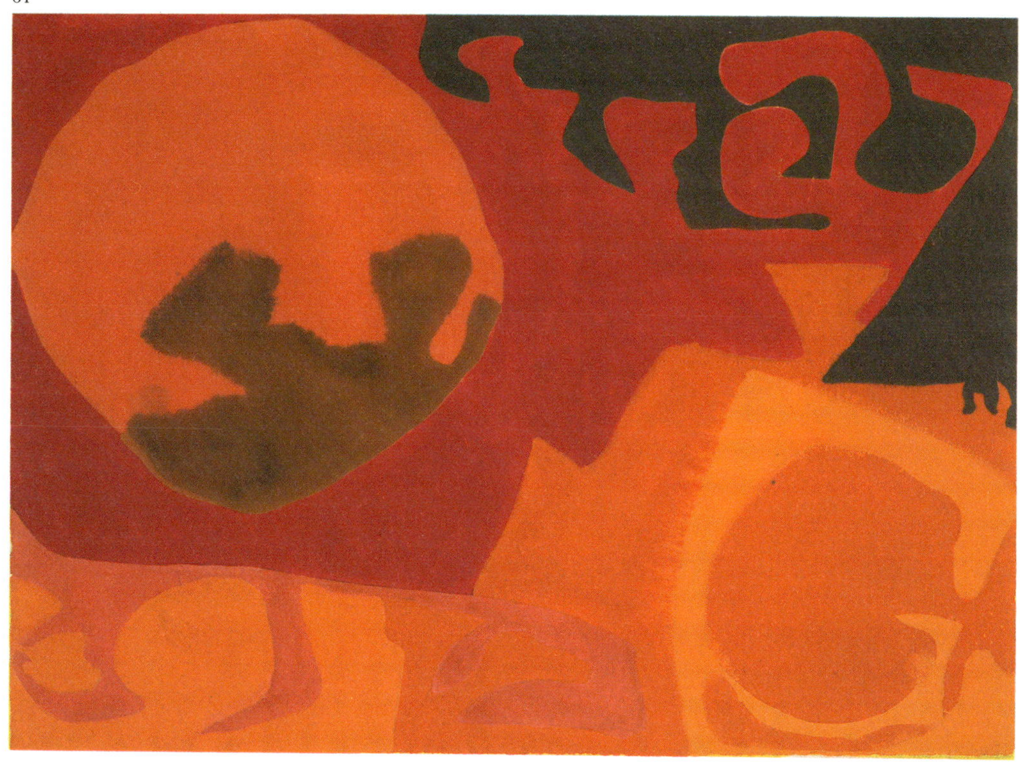

61 **Patrick Heron** born 1920
*Complex Carmines and Cadmiums with Brown
(Luminous Disc)* 1968
gouache on paper $22\frac{1}{8} \times 31$ in ($56 \cdot 2 \times 78 \cdot 8$ cm)

Patrick Heron's painting is concerned with colour and the excitement – the optical aliveness – achieved when colours are juxtaposed in particular ways. Hence the ostensibly plain matter-of-factness (with a little alliterative lyricism somehow creeping in) of the title of this gouache (done during a year when larger scale work was out of the question since he was recovering from a canoeing accident). At this time the boundary lines between colours in the paintings were becoming increasingly complicated providing a growing richness of effect.

Bought 1968

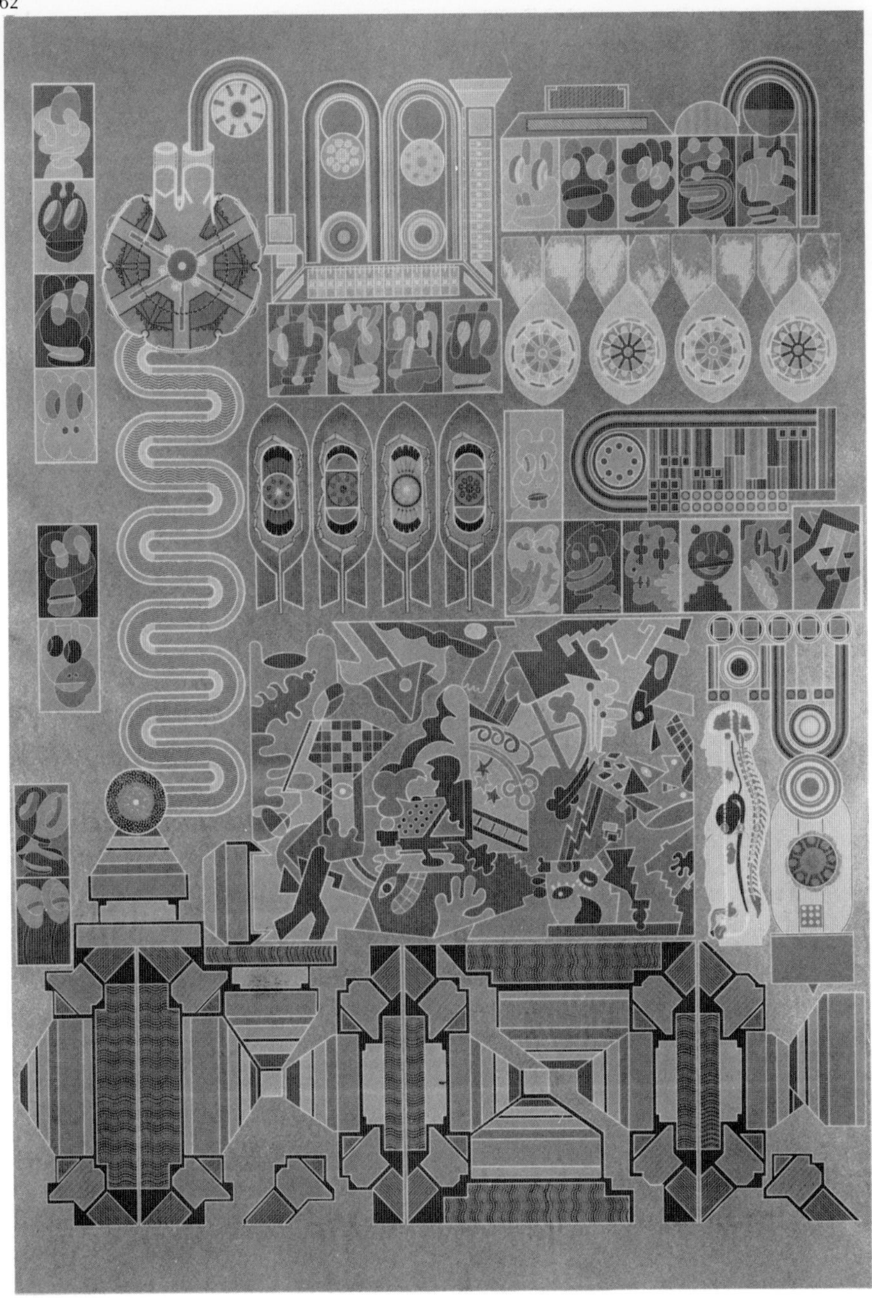

62 Eduardo Paolozzi born 1920
Who's afraid of Sugar Pink and Lime Green?
1971
silkscreen print $58\frac{1}{8} \times 40\frac{3}{4}$ in
($147 \cdot 5 \times 103 \cdot 5$ cm)
signed and dated

Drawing, as this artist so often does, on a
multiplicity of visual source material – from
Walt Disney to machine parts to anatomical
illustration to architectural design, the wealth
of allusion in this print repays prolonged
attention. The title mocks current 'fine art'
attitudes; yet the craftsmanship in the
printing proclaims the artist's belief in the
marvellous magical possibilities to be found
in the landscape of modern living.

Given by the Artist, 1977

63 **Keith Milow** born 1945
71-A1 1971
acrylic on card $19\frac{1}{4} \times 29\frac{3}{4}$ in ($49 \times 78 \cdot 5$ cm)
signed and dated

This is one of a set of works made by drawing through creamy acrylic paint with a decorator's comb. Each drawing in the set was striated in this way at a progressively steeper angle, derived from a graph curve, in its turn derived from a drawing made from a sculpture. Keith Milow was interested in the transformation of the meaning of images through this kind of obscuring process. Side by side with this rational programme runs a liking for the physical nature of materials–the sensuousness of the creamy paint over the silvered ground.

Given by the Yorkshire Arts Association, 1978

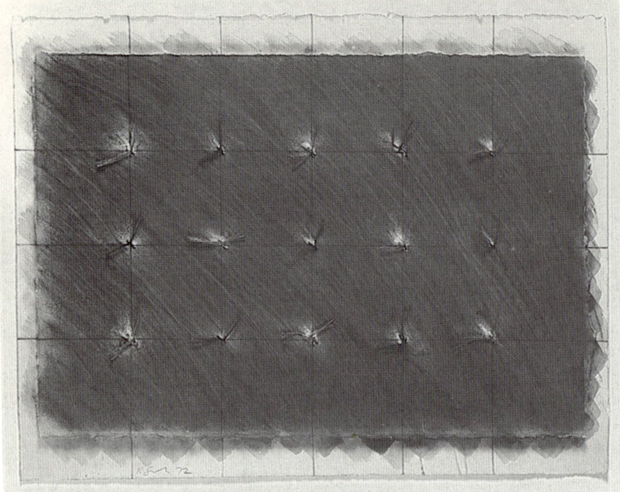

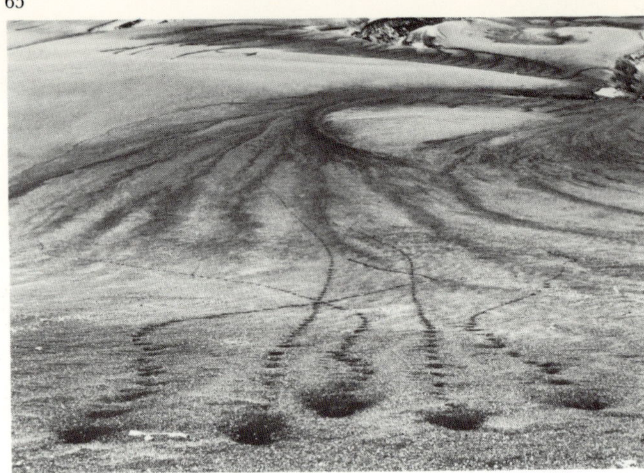

64 **Richard Smith** born 1931
Untitled (15 knots) 1972
watercolour on paper with string $23\frac{1}{4} \times 30\frac{1}{2}$ in
$(59 \times 77 \cdot 5$ cm)
signed and dated

Up to this period Richard Smith's
paintings – which were three-dimensional,
actually made on curved stretchers – had
depended on intricate but concealed
carpentry. In the paintings first shown in 1972
he completely reversed this conception and
the stretchers of his new paintings were light
in weight and apparent to the spectator. In the
drawings of that period the same principle
operates – knotted string holds the paper to its
ground and both are made to play their part in
the articulation of the drawing; colour,
ground and structure are clearly differentiated
and the order of making the work can be
easily deduced by the viewer.

Bought by the Leeds Art Collections Fund, 1972

65 **Richard Long** born 1945
Five Stones, Iceland 1974
photograph 20×30 in $(51 \times 76$ cm)

Richard Long makes sculptures actually in
the landscape as well as in galleries, usually in
remote and inaccessible places. For these very
private works photography is a way of letting
the public into the secret as it were. The
landscape sculptures are most often ordered
arrangements of elements of the landscape
found on site – rocks, stones, driftwood,
branches – set in circles or straight lines. *Five
Stones* which was made in Iceland differs from
those works in that chance plays a larger part:
it was made by setting five boulders – found *in
situ* – to roll down the side of a volcano; the
tracks they made constitute the work and
these were dictated by gravity and the
contours of the land itself.

Bought 1975

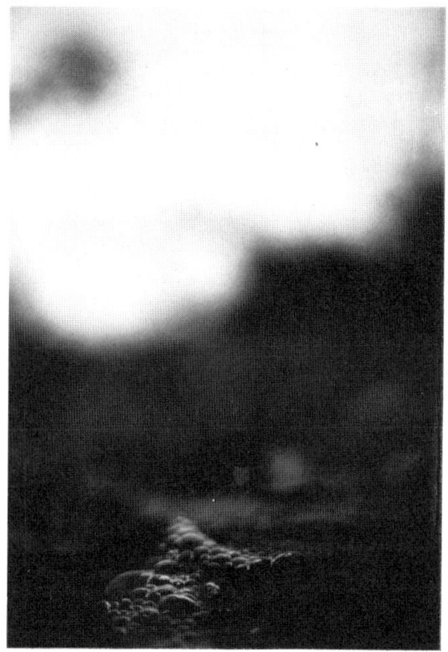 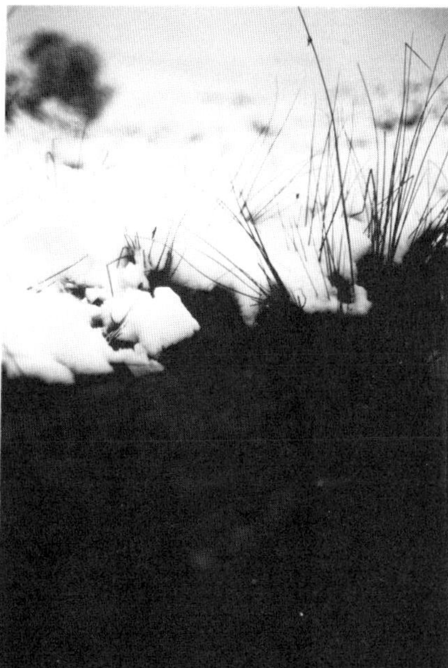 

66 John Hilliard born 1945
December Water 1976
three photographs with text, each
photograph 22½ × 15 in (57 × 38 cm)

John Hilliard has been using photographs in
his work since before 1970, when he began to
be interested in the relationship between the
sculptures he was making, and the
photographs of them which were more
widely seen (in magazines, for example) than
the actual work. In his recent work he has
been presenting sets of exactly the same view
as seen by the camera but – through
alterations in the photographic process –
offering quite different images. This
procedure both comments on the traditional
view of the camera as a mechanical device
which 'does not lie' and alerts us to our own
methods of perception.

December Water was made during a year spent
in Northumberland on a Northern Arts
Fellowship in 1976.

Bought 1979

Further reading

Wendy Baron, *The Camden Town Group*, 1979
Scolar Press

British Council and Commune di Milano,
Arte Inglese Oggi, catalogue of an exhibition
held at the Palazzo Reale, Milan 1976 (English
text)

Richard Cork, *Vorticism and its Allies*, 1974
Hayward Gallery, London, Arts Council of
Great Britain

Sir John Rothenstein, *British Art since 1900*,
1962 Phaidon Press

Richard Shone, *Bloomsbury Portraits*, 1976
Phaidon Press

Richard Shone, *The Century of Change*, 1977
Phaidon Press

We regret that no. 20 will only be exhibited at
Bath, Huddersfield, Coventry and Preston.
Similarly, nos. 35 & 36 will only be shown at
Bath, Huddersfield, Coventry, Lincoln and
Bolton. No. 16 will not join the exhibition
before Huddersfield.